™

Get Wise!

MASTERING
Math
SKILLS

by David Frieder

with Stephanie Smith

THOMSON
★
PETERSON'S

Australia • Canada • Mexico • Singapore • Spain • United Kingdom • United States

D0206872

THOMSON
PETERSON'S

About The Thomson Corporation and Peterson's

With revenues of US$7.2 billion, The Thomson Corporation (www.thomson.com) is a leading global provider of integrated information solutions for business, education, and professional customers. Its Learning businesses and brands (www.thomsonlearning.com) serve the needs of individuals, learning institutions, and corporations with products and services for both traditional and distributed learning.

Peterson's, part of The Thomson Corporation, is one of the nation's most respected providers of lifelong learning online resources, software, reference guides, and books. The Education Supersite[SM] at www.petersons.com—the Internet's most heavily traveled education resource—has searchable databases and interactive tools for contacting U.S.-accredited institutions and programs. In addition, Peterson's serves more than 105 million education consumers annually.

Get Wise! Mastering Math Skills is adapted from *Mathematics Workbook for the SAT* by David Frieder.

For more information, contact Peterson's, 2000 Lenox Drive, Lawrenceville, NJ 08648; 800-338-3282; or find us on the World Wide Web at www.petersons.com/about.

COPYRIGHT © 2002 Peterson's, a division of Thomson Learning, Inc. Thomson Learning™ is a trademark used herein under license.

Get Wise!™ is a trademark of Peterson's, a division of Thomson Learning, Inc.

ALL RIGHTS RESERVED. No part of this work covered by the copyright herein may be reproduced or used in any form or by any means—graphic, electronic, or mechanical, including photocopying, recording, taping, Web distribution, or information storage and retrieval systems—without the prior written permission of the publisher.

For permission to use material from this text or product, contact us by
Phone: 800-730-2214
Fax: 800-730-2215
Web: www.thomsonrights.com

ISBN: 0-7689-1076-5

Printed in Canada

10 9 8 7 6 5 4 3 2 1   04 03 02

Contents

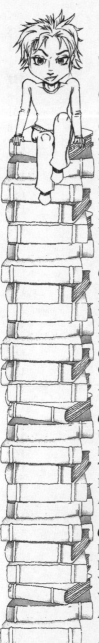

introduction

Welcome to *Math Wise*, a swan dive into the world of math. Sounds like fun, right? Well, before you judge, ditch that pocket protector, stomp on that graphing calculator, and throw out any thoughts like "math is too hard," because you've never seen a study aid like this before.

Sure, we'll have instructions and answers and even some problems. But before you look away in disgust and fling this five-ounce book filled with fractions, decimals, and geometry at the nearest annoying relative or classmate, give it a chance. Remember, we who write this also did our time in those brick-walled funhouses called *schools*, with math teachers who went on and on about isolating variables and keeping a neat notebook. Our goal is to show you that math is easier than they made it look.

As we walk you along the path of the basics, through the maze of algebra, and across the planes of geometry, we'll show you how to make the most of your time and brainpower.

Can't see the point in learning math because you think that you won't use it too often when you leave school? Think again, oh-student-about-to-succeed-in-life. There are numerous daily events that require a grasp of the math world. I'll bet that hours of your week are consumed with either one or both of the two most interesting pastimes to a teenager: sports and shopping. Well, statistics and percents are used quite often to succeed at both. And these math concepts

v

include tons of other interesting areas like averages, rates, ratios, proportions, comparisons, fractions, decimals, and the old stand-bys like addition, subtraction, multiplication, and division.

Now that you think about it, we'll bet you can remember doing some form of math today. Did you get up late only to look at the alarm clock to calculate how late you could be before missing the bus? Did you cook dinner and have to read the line for a fraction of a cup of water or milk? So you see, math is all around us.

Back to the book. You'll see that there are 10 chapters, and each chapter concentrates on a different concept. Math builds on itself; so if you think you understand how to add or subtract fractions, don't just jump to Chapter 4. There is valuable information you will miss in chapters 1 through 3 that you may need as you progress through the book.

So, you are better off starting at Chapter 1. If it's too easy for you, GOOD. That's supposed to be the easy chapter. That's why it's at the beginning. Do the exercises, reward yourself with some candy or a nap, and when you're ready, continue through the book.

If you are having a specific problem in school with a specific area, feel free to practice in that chapter only. We're not going to send the Math Police after you for skipping around. But we do suggest that this book is most helpful if you digest it all, kind of like cough medicine—a tiny sip won't make the pain go away, so you have to take a full dose to benefit.

So if you're ready to learn—at least read a few more pages so that the parental units will feel proud (and feed you tonight)—turn to Chapter 1.

Best of luck, and we hope that you *Get Wise!*

chapter 1

The Operations

SO, WHY DO I NEED MATH?

Think math is just another four-letter word? Think again. Knowledge of math is handy in many real-life situations, like when you need to:

★ Calculate a good tip to impress your date

★ Determine whether 20% off is a good discount on a cool new skirt

★ Find out just how much of your paycheck you blow on new video games

Face the facts, math is one subject they teach you in school that you actually *do* use.

1

Get Wise! Mastering Math Skills   *www.petersons.com*

Math? I haven't used math in weeks, well, days . . . no, that's not true either because the fact that I'm counting backward in my head to think about it probably counts as math. Now, that's not fair!

GETTING IT TOGETHER: ADDITION

In math, we add numbers, called *addends*, and create *sums*, which is what math people call the answers to addition problems. To solve an addition problem, you must line up the addends, keeping the numbers in the ones column straight, one below the other.

Example: Find the sum of 403, 37, 8314, and 5.

$$
\begin{array}{r}
\overset{+1}{4}03 \\
37 \\
8314 \\
+\quad 4 \\
\hline
8758
\end{array}
$$

Solution:

(Since the numbers in the ones column add up to 18, you must carry the 1 (heavy, huh?) over into the tens column.)

Numbers we add are called ADDENDS?
Geez, could the math people get
LESS creative?

Get Wise!

Seems pretty simple, right? Now try these five examples and see if the answers you get match the ones we got.

1. Find the sum of 360, 4352, 87, and 205.
   (A) 5013
   (D) 6004
   (B) 5004
   (E) 6013
   (C) 5003

If you look closely, you'll notice that the answer choices are similar. This happens all the time and it's annoying. It's like the teachers KNOW the mistakes we might make and they try to trick us! This is why I try to trick them *back* and do my adding twice—once by going down the columns and then by adding up.

2. Find the sum of 4321, 2143, 1234, and 3412.
   (A) 12,110
   (D) 11,111
   (B) 11,011
   (E) 11,110
   (C) 11,101

3. Add 56 + 321 + 8 + 42.
   (A) 427
   (D) 417
   (B) 437
   (E) 527
   (C) 517

4. Add 99 + 88 + 77 + 66 + 55.
   (A) 384
   (D) 375
   (B) 485
   (E) 376
   (C) 385

5. Add 1212 + 2323 + 3434 + 4545 + 5656.
    (A) 17,171   (D) 17,280
    (B) 17,170   (E) 17,270
    (C) 17,160

How wise? Check your answers on page 24.

TAKING IT APART: SUBTRACTION

Subtraction is removing numbers from other ones. It's fairly simple. All you have to remember is that you have to line them up (like in addition) and if the number on top is smaller, you must borrow from the column to the left. For example, in

$$
\begin{array}{r}
54 \\
-38 \\
\hline
\end{array}
$$

it's obvious that you can't take 8 away from 4 because 4 is smaller. So, you need to change the 5 to a 4 and make the 4 a 14. What you're really doing is borrowing from the tens column (the 5 in 54 means there are 5 tens, or 50) and giving to the units column.

$$
\begin{array}{r}
{\scriptstyle 4\ 14} \\
\cancel{5}\ \cancel{4} \\
-3\ 8 \\
\hline
1\ 6
\end{array}
$$

The answer in subtraction is called the *difference*. This is basically telling us that the difference between 54 and 38 is 16.

Yeah, I learned this when I was little. Of course, most of my teachers now let me use a calculator, so it's not like I remember this borrowing concept or anything. I suppose it's good to know if I forget my calculator and that nerd who always lets me borrow his stuff is absent or something.

Sometimes subtraction requires you to borrow across more than one column:

$$503$$
$$-267$$

In the above problem, you can't subtract 7 from 3, and you can't borrow from 0! To solve it, you must change the 5 into a 4 (this is the hundreds column now) and give the hundred to the 0, making the tens column a 10.

$$\overset{4 \ \ 10}{\cancel{5}\cancel{0}3}$$
$$-2\,6\,7$$

Then you have to change the 10 to a 9 in order to make the 3 into a 13. It might sound complicated, but with practice it becomes second nature.

$$\overset{4 \ \ \overset{9}{\cancel{10}} \ 13}{\cancel{5}\cancel{0}\cancel{3}}$$
$$-2\,6\,7$$
$$\overline{2\,3\,6}$$

Just remember to write the 1s and cross out any number you don't use in the final problem (like the 10). Keeping organized is the key to successful math.

Get Wise!

Try these problems to see if you really understand the concept of subtraction.

1. Subtract 803 from 952.
   (A) 248
   (B) 148
   (C) 249
   (D) 149
   (E) 147

2. From the sum of 837 and 415, subtract 1035.
   (A) 217
   (B) 216
   (C) 326
   (D) 227
   (E) 226

Great, it's already getting tricky. *Sum* was from the addition section—this is supposed to be subtraction. *Note to Chi*: Math people combine lots of ideas to confuse me and throw me off track. I'm gonna have to remember that for later.

3. From 1872 subtract the sum of 76 and 43.
   (A) 1754
   (B) 1838
   (C) 1753
   (D) 1839
   (E) 1905

4. Find the difference between 237 and 732.
   (A) 496
   (B) 495
   (C) 486
   (D) 405
   (E) 497

5. By how much does the sum of 612 and 315 exceed the sum of 451 and 283?
   (A) 294
   (B) 1661
   (C) 293
   (D) 197
   (E) 193

How wise? Check your answers on page 25.

MULTIPLY MANIA

In multiplication, the answer is called a *product*. The numbers you multiply are called *factors* of the product. To multiply numbers with two or more digits, you have to line them up and keep them organized, just like in addition and subtraction. For example, to multiply 537 by 72, first you multiply it by 2 and then by 7. Actually, the 7 stands for 70 so you have to keep a 0 in the units place in your work for the second multiplication. Watch:

$$
\begin{array}{r}
537 \\
\times \quad 72 \\
\hline
1074 \\
+37590 \\
\hline
38664
\end{array}
$$

You add the two multiplications (the 2 and the 7) and get your final answer.

Oh geez, where is my calculator? This is already starting to hurt my head. 7 times 2 is 14, carry the 1. Sounds kinda familiar. Math is like shopping, with all this borrowing and carrying. Except I *like* shopping.

Got it? Now you have to try it with three-digit numbers, too.

$$
\begin{array}{r}
372 \\
\times \quad 461 \\
\hline
372 \\
22320 \\
+ 148800 \\
\hline
171492
\end{array}
$$

See, that wasn't too bad, was it? How about finding the following products and then check your answers to make sure you're moving along with all this.

Get Wise!

Find the products for the problems below.

1. 526 multiplied by 317
   - (A) 156,742
   - (B) 165,742
   - (C) 166,742
   - (D) 166,748
   - (E) 166,708

2. 8347 multiplied by 62
   - (A) 517,514
   - (B) 517,414
   - (C) 517,504
   - (D) 517,114
   - (E) 617,114

3. 705 multiplied by 89
   - (A) 11,985
   - (B) 52,745
   - (C) 62,705
   - (D) 62,745
   - (E) 15,121

4. 437 multiplied by 607
   - (A) 265,259
   - (B) 265,219
   - (C) 265,359
   - (D) 265,059
   - (E) 262,059

5. 798 multiplied by 450
   - (A) 358,600
   - (B) 359,100
   - (C) 71,820
   - (D) 358,100
   - (E) 360,820

How wise? Check your answers on page 25.

DIVIDE AND CONQUER

Congratulations! You've made it through addition, subtraction, and multiplication—which leaves only division to complete the four basic operations.

Unfortunately, there is some more vocabulary here to digest:

★ The number being divided is called the *dividend*.

★ The number you are dividing by is called the *divisor*.

★ The answer in division is called the *quotient*.

★ If the quotient is not an *integer* (it doesn't divide in neatly), you have a *remainder*.

What's this? *Vocabulary* in MATH? No way did I sign up for this! At least "dividend" and "divisor" sound like you're doing division—but quotient? I didn't even know you could put all those vowels together and form a word.

Simply put, division can be neat: 18 divided by 6 is 3. And you can check that by multiplying: 3 times 6 is 18. Or division can be messy: 19 divided by 6 is 3 remainder 1. When you have a remainder, you will write it as a fraction. Just make sure you use the remainder as the numerator and the divisor as the denominator. So:

$$\frac{19}{6} = 3\frac{1}{6}$$

Division by a single-digit divisor looks like this:

$$
\begin{array}{r}
9724 \\
6\overline{)58344} \\
\underline{54} \\
43 \\
\underline{42} \\
14 \\
\underline{12} \\
24 \\
\underline{24} \\
0
\end{array}
$$

Great! Division has adding, subtracting, and multiplying all mixed in it! Math is so filled with that one-on-top-of-the-other principle. It's like when I invite a person over to watch "Buffy," but she doesn't know the backstory because she's been on, like, Mars, and hasn't watched it, and I have to explain.

Get Wise!

Division probably looks harder than it is. Try the following problems to see if you understand.

1. Divide 391 by 23.
   - (A) 10
   - (B) 12
   - (C) 17
   - (D) 100
   - (E) 170

2. Divide 49,523,436 by 9.
   - (A) 6,502,603
   - (B) 55,264
   - (C) 5,502,604
   - (D) 6,502,604
   - (E) 5,502,603

3. Find 4,832 ÷ 15.
   - (A) 322
   - (B) $322\frac{2}{15}$
   - (C) 324
   - (D) $322\frac{1}{2}$
   - (E) 3,222

4. Divide 42,098 by 7.
   - (A) 6,014
   - (B) 614
   - (C) 62
   - (D) 60,014
   - (E) 6,000

5. Find 333,180 ÷ 617.
   - (A) 541
   - (B) 542
   - (C) 539
   - (D) 540
   - (E) 545

How wise? Check your answers on page 26.

DECIMALS HAVE A POINT

"Without precise calculations, we could fly right through a star or bounce too close to a Supernova and that'd end your trip real quick, wouldn't it?"

—Han Solo, *Star Wars*

We use decimals to make life more precise. Wouldn't you rather eat junk food that was 99.9999% tasty than just plain old 99% tasty?

When dealing with decimals, the most important concept to understand is that they must all line up by their decimal points. Keep these in line, and you'll have an easy time adding or subtracting.

Example: Find the sum of 8.4, .37, and 2.641.

Solution:

$$
\begin{array}{r}
8.4 \\
.37 \\
+\,2.641 \\
\hline
11.411
\end{array}
$$

Simple, see? Do the same with subtraction.

Example: Find the difference between 48.3 and 27.56.

Solution:

$$
\begin{array}{r}
{}^{7}\,{}^{12}\,{}^{10} \\
4\,8.3\,0 \\
-\,27.5\,6 \\
\hline
2\,0.7\,4
\end{array}
$$

See how we filled in the zero in 48.3 to make it have the same amount of numbers as 27.56? You have to do that in order to perform the borrowing that you learned in subtraction. Don't worry, decimals can have as many zeros to the right of the last number after the decimal as you want. It won't change the property of the decimal.

Get Wise!

Can you successfully add and subtract decimals? Find out for yourself.

1. From the sum of .65, 4.2, 17.63, and 8, subtract 12.7.
   - (A) 9.78
   - (B) 17.68
   - (C) 17.78
   - (D) 17.79
   - (E) 18.78

2. Find the sum of .837, .12, 52.3, and .354.
   - (A) 53.503
   - (B) 53.611
   - (C) 53.601
   - (D) 54.601
   - (E) 54.611

3. From 561.8 subtract 34.75.
   - (A) 537.05
   - (B) 537.15
   - (C) 527.15
   - (D) 527.04
   - (E) 527.05

4. From 53.72 subtract the sum of 4.81 and 17.5.
   - (A) 31.86
   - (B) 31.41
   - (C) 41.03
   - (D) 66.41
   - (E) 41.86

5. Find the difference between 100 and 52.18.
   - (A) 37.82
   - (B) 47.18
   - (C) 47.92
   - (D) 47.82
   - (E) 37.92

How wise? Check your answers on page 27.

Multiplying Decimals

There is no hard way to explain this. You multiply a decimal as you would an integer. Then you count up your decimal places and place them in the answer.

Example: Multiply .375 by .42

Solution:

$$
\begin{array}{r}
.375 \\
\times\ \underline{.42} \\
750 \\
+\underline{15000} \\
.15750
\end{array}
$$

Since you have three numbers after the decimal point in the first number and two numbers after the decimal point in the second number, you put the decimal five total places to the left of your answer.

Multiplying by multiples of 10 is easier. Just count the zeros and put the decimal that many places to the right of the number you're multiplying.

Count the zeros. Now you're talking. I wish I could practice counting the zeros in my bank account.

Here are two examples:

$4.5 \times 100 = 450$ (two places to the right)

$56.78 \times 10,000 = 567,800$ (four places to the right)

Get Wise!

Try the following decimal multiplication problems.

1. $437 \times .24 =$
   (A) 1.0488   (D) 1048.8
   (B) 10.488   (E) 10,488
   (C) 104.88

2. $5.06 \times .7 =$
   (A) .3542   (D) 3.542
   (B) .392   (E) 35.42
   (C) 3.92

3. $83 \times 1.5 =$
   (A) 12.45   (D) 124.5
   (B) 49.8   (E) 1.245
   (C) 498

4. $.7314 \times 100 =$
   (A) .007314   (D) 73.14
   (B) .07314   (E) 731.4
   (C) 7.314

5. $.0008 \times 4.3 =$
   (A) .000344   (D) 0.344
   (B) .00344   (E) 3.44
   (C) .0344

How wise? Check your answers on page 28.

Dividing Decimals

The main thing to remember about dividing decimals is that you have to change the divisor to a whole number. Since decimals are so small, dividing by one results in a large number and it's easiest to make this adjustment first.

Example: $.06\overline{)2.592}$

Solution: You must change .06 to a 6 by moving the decimal two places to the right. Once you do this, you must also move the decimal of the number you're dividing into two places to the right. So,

the problem becomes: $6\overline{)259.2}$

Dividing by 10 or 100 or 1000 is easy. Count the zeros and move the decimal that many places to the left, the opposite of multiplication. Here are two examples:

542 divided by 10 is 54.2.

1380 divided by 100 is 13.80.

Get Wise!

Try the following decimal division problems.

1. Divide 4.3 by 100.
- (A) .0043
- (B) 0.043
- (C) 0.43
- (D) 43
- (E) 430

2. Find the quotient when 4.371 is divided by .3.
- (A) 0.1457
- (B) 1.457
- (C) 14.57
- (D) 145.7
- (E) 1457

3. Divide .64 by .4.
   (A) .0016   (D) 1.6
   (B) 0.016   (E) 16
   (C) 0.16

4. Find $.12 \div \dfrac{2}{.5}$.

   (A) 4.8   (D) 0.3
   (B) 48   (E) 3
   (C) .03

5. Find $\dfrac{10.2}{.03} \div \dfrac{1.7}{.1}$.

   (A) .02   (D) 20
   (B) 0.2   (E) 200
   (C) 2

How wise? Check your answers on page 29.

MATH LAWS

"We live in a society of laws. Why do you think I took you to all those Police Academy movies? For fun? Well I didn't hear anybody laughin', did you?"

—Homer Simpson

Yes, math has many laws. And in order for math to be useful, we have to obey them. Sometimes there are many different ways to solve a problem, but there are basic rules that will always apply.

Commutative. Associative. Distributive. Identity. Order of Operations. If these words are causing the cobwebs in your brain to rattle, don't worry. A quick refresher will help you regain clarity and composure.

★ *Commutative* means the order doesn't change the answer. Addition and multiplication are commutative: you can do the problem in any order you want and still get the right answer (yes!). Watch:

$$4 + 7 = 7 + 4$$
$$5 \times 3 = 3 \times 5$$

★ *Associative* is when the grouping doesn't matter. Again, addition and multiplication are the only operations where this works. Watch:

$$(3 + 4) + 5 = 3 + (4 + 5)$$
$$(3 \cdot 4) \cdot 5 = 3 \cdot (4 \cdot 5)$$

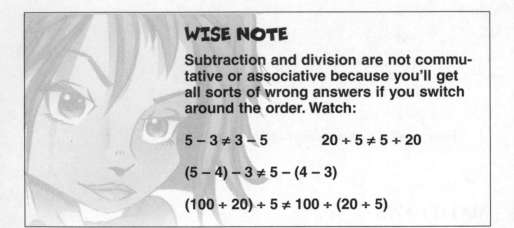

WISE NOTE

Subtraction and division are not commutative or associative because you'll get all sorts of wrong answers if you switch around the order. Watch:

$$5 - 3 \neq 3 - 5 \qquad 20 \div 5 \neq 5 \div 20$$

$$(5 - 4) - 3 \neq 5 - (4 - 3)$$

$$(100 \div 20) \div 5 \neq 100 \div (20 \div 5)$$

★ *Distributive* is a property of only multiplication. This says that 3(5 + 2 + 4) can be done two ways:

1) Add the numbers in parentheses and multiply by 3,

2) OR distribute the 3 to each number, multiplying 3×5, 3×2, and 3×4, and then add up those three numbers.

Obviously, it's not hard to see that in this case it's a lot easier to just add up the number in parentheses first, but this can come in handy as a concept in bigger and harder problems.

★ *Identity* numbers mean that when you use them, nothing happens. In addition, identity is found with a 0. Any number plus 0 is equal to that number; you're not changing the identities of any numbers involved. In multiplication, identity is 1, since any number times 1 is equal to that number.

★ *Order of Operations*—When several operations are found in a problem, it's important that we do them in a certain order. You may have learned PEMDAS, or "Please Excuse My Dear Aunt Sally," as a memory trick. Simply put, it means first do Parentheses and Exponents, then Multiplication and Division, and lastly Addition and Subtraction.

Example: Find $5 \cdot 4 + 6 \div 2 - 16 \div 4$.

Solution: If you remember to first do multiplication and division over addition and subtraction, then your parentheses (showing priority of order) would look like this: $(5 \cdot 4) + (6 \div 2) - (16 \div 4)$, which is $20 + 3 - 4 = 19$.

OK, so I understand that certain rules only apply to certain math operations. Just like life. Is nothing simple?

Get Wise!

Try the following problems to see what you've learned about the laws of math!

1. Find $8 + 4 \div 2 + 6 \cdot 3 - 1$.
   (A) 35   (D) 27
   (B) 47   (E) 88
   (C) 43

2. $16 \div 4 + 2 \cdot 3 + 2 - 8 \div 2$.
   (A) 6   (D) 4
   (B) 8   (E) 10
   (C) 2

Match each equation in the left-hand column with the law it illustrates from the right hand column.

3. $475 \cdot 1 = 475$ (A) Identity for Addition

4. $75 + 12 = 12 + 75$ (B) Associative Law of Multiplication

5. $32(12 + 8) = 32(12) + 32(8)$ (C) Identity for Multiplication

6. $378 + 0 = 378$ (D) Distributive Law of Multiplication over Addition

7. $(7 \cdot 5) \cdot 2 = 7 \cdot (5 \cdot 2)$ (E) Commutative Law of Addition

How wise? Check your answers on page 29.

ESTIMATING

On many tests, such as the SAT, time is a factor. Estimating can help you save precious time so you can concentrate on more difficult problems.

> I can think of PLENTY more difficult problems I could concentrate on, and believe me, none has anything to do whatsoever with math!

Example: The product of 498 and 103 is

   (A) 5124   (D) 31,674

   (B) 501,294   (E) 817,324

   (C) 51,294

Solution: If you have a calculator, sure this is easy, but what if you don't have the electronic help? Just estimate: 498 is about 500. 103 is about 100. So the product is about (500) (100) or 50,000 (just move the decimal point two places to the right when multiplying by 100). Which answer is closest? The correct answer is (C).

Try another one:

Example: Which of the following is closest to the value of $4831 \cdot \dfrac{710}{2314}$?

   (A) 83   (D) 3140

   (B) 425   (E) 6372

   (C) 1600

Solution: Estimating, we have $\left(\dfrac{(5000)(700)}{2000}\right)$. That's the same as 3,500,000 divided by 2000. Knock off three 0s on top and bottom to simplify and you're left with $\dfrac{3500}{2}$ or 1750. Choice (C) is the closest answer.

Get Wise!

Try the following estimation problems to see if you have the hang of it.

1. $\dfrac{483+1875}{119}$

   (A) 2
   (B) 10
   (C) 20
   (D) 50
   (E) 100

2. $\dfrac{6017 \cdot 312}{364+618}$

   (A) 18
   (B) 180
   (C) 1800
   (D) 18,000
   (E) 180,000

3. $\dfrac{783+491}{1532-879}$

   (A) .02
   (B) .2
   (C) 2
   (D) 20
   (E) 200

How wise? Check your answers on page 29.

A Word to the Wise

Addition, Subtraction, Multiplication, and Division: The Vocabulary

★ *Addends* add together to create *sums*.

★ Answers in subtraction are called *differences*.

★ Multiplication answers are called *products*.

★ *Dividends* are divided by *divisors* to get *quotients*.

Addition, Subtraction, Multiplication, and Division: The Rules

★ *Commutative Property* means that the order doesn't matter. This is found in addition and multiplication.

$$5 + 4 = 4 + 5$$

★ *Associative Property* means you can group it any way. This is found in addition and multiplication.

$$(5 \times 4) \times 3 = 5 \times (4 \times 3)$$

★ *Identity Property* of 0 is in addition: 0 can be added to any number without changing the number.

★ *Identity Property* of 1 is in multiplication: Any number multiplied by 1 stays the same.

★ *Order of Operations* is **PEMDAS:**

a. First you must do the work in **Parentheses** and clear the **Exponents.**

b. Then do **Multiplication** and **Division.**

c. **Addition** and **Subtraction** are done last.

WISE POINTS

* In addition and subtraction, you must *line up digits by columns and decimals.*
* Sometimes subtraction requires *borrowing.* Keep your crossed-out numbers *organized.*
* *Remainders* are usually written in fraction form.
* To *divide* by a decimal, *change it into an integer* and *move the decimal* over the same amount of places in the dividend.
* *Estimating* saves time.

ANSWERS TO CHAPTER 1: PRACTICE EXERCISES

Addition (Page 3)

1. **(B)**
$$
\begin{array}{r}
360 \\
4352 \\
87 \\
+205 \\
\hline
5004
\end{array}
$$

2. **(E)**
$$
\begin{array}{r}
4321 \\
2143 \\
1234 \\
+3412 \\
\hline
11{,}110
\end{array}
$$

3. **(A)**
$$
\begin{array}{r}
56 \\
321 \\
8 \\
+42 \\
\hline
427
\end{array}
$$

4. **(C)**
$$
\begin{array}{r}
99 \\
88 \\
77 \\
66 \\
+55 \\
\hline
385
\end{array}
$$

5. **(B)**   1212
2323
3434
4545
+<u>5656</u>
17,170

Subtraction (Page 5)

1. **(D)**   9 $\overset{4\ 12}{\cancel{5}\ \cancel{2}}$
−8 0 3
1 4 9

2. **(A)**   837
+ 415
1252

12$\overset{4\ 12}{\cancel{5}\ \cancel{2}}$
−10 3 5
2 1 7

3. **(C)**   76
+ 43
119

18$\overset{6\ 12}{\cancel{7}\ \cancel{2}}$
− 1 1 9
1 7 5 3

4. **(B)** $\overset{6\ 12\ 12}{\cancel{7}\ \cancel{3}\ \cancel{2}}$
−2 3 7
4 9 5

5. **(E)**   612
+ 315
927

451
+ 283
734

$\overset{8\ 12}{\cancel{9}\ \cancel{2}}$7
−7 3 4
1 9 3

Multiplication (Page 8)

1. **(C)**   526
× 317
3682
5260
157800
166,742

2. **(A)**
$$
\begin{array}{r}
8347 \\
\times\ \ 62 \\
\hline
16694 \\
500820 \\
\hline
517,514
\end{array}
$$

3. **(D)**
$$
\begin{array}{r}
705 \\
\times\ \ 89 \\
\hline
6345 \\
56400 \\
\hline
62,745
\end{array}
$$

4. **(A)**
$$
\begin{array}{r}
437 \\
\times\ \ 607 \\
\hline
3059 \\
262200 \\
\hline
265,259
\end{array}
$$

5. **(B)**
$$
\begin{array}{r}
798 \\
\times\ \ 450 \\
\hline
39900 \\
319200 \\
\hline
359,100
\end{array}
$$

Division (Page 11)

1. **(C)**
$$
\begin{array}{r}
17 \\
23\overline{)391} \\
23 \\
\hline
161 \\
161 \\
\hline
0
\end{array}
$$

2. **(C)**
$$
9\overline{)49,523,436} \quad \text{(quotient } 5,502,604)
$$

3. **(B)**
$$
\begin{array}{r}
322 \text{ Remainder } 2 \\
15\overline{)4832} \\
45 \\
\hline
33 \\
30 \\
\hline
32 \\
30 \\
\hline
2
\end{array}
$$

4. **(A)**
$$
7\overline{)42098} \quad \text{(quotient } 6014)
$$

5. **(D)** Want a trick? Look at the answer choices. The quotient will be multiplied by 617 and get 333,180 as an answer. So the quotient must end in a 0 when it's multiplied by 617! Geniuses, aren't we? This can only be choice (D), since 617 times choice (A) would end in 7, choice (B) would end in 4, choice (C) in 3, and choice (E) in 5. Wiser people work less!

Decimals: Adding and Subtracting (Page 13)

1. **(C)**

```
  .65
 4.2
17.63
+8.
─────
30.48
```

```
2 9 14
3 0 . 4 8
-1 2 . 7 0
─────────
1 7 . 7 8
```

2. **(B)**

```
  .837
  .12
52.3
+  .354
──────
53.611
```

3. **(E)**

```
5 11 7 10
5 6 1 . 8 0
-    3 4 . 7 5
───────────
5 2 7 . 0 5
```

4. **(B)**

```
 4.81
+17.50
──────
22.31
```

```
53.72
-22.31
──────
31.41
```

5. **(D)**

```
0 9 9  9 10
1 0 0 . 0 0
-   5 2 . 1 8
───────────
4 7 . 8 2
```

Decimals: Multiplying (Page 15)

1. **(C)**

$$
\begin{array}{r}
437 \\
\times\ .24 \\
\hline
1748 \\
8740 \\
\hline
104.88
\end{array}
$$

2. **(D)**

$$
\begin{array}{r}
5.06 \\
\times\ .7 \\
\hline
3.542
\end{array}
$$

3. **(D)**

$$
\begin{array}{r}
83 \\
\times 1.5 \\
\hline
415 \\
830 \\
\hline
124.5
\end{array}
$$

4. **(D)** Just move the decimal point two places to the right!

5. **(B)**

$$
\begin{array}{r}
.0008 \\
\times\ 4.3 \\
\hline
24 \\
320 \\
\hline
.00344
\end{array}
$$

Decimals: Division (Page 16)

1. **(B)** Just move the decimal point two places to the left!

2. **(C)** $.3\overline{)4.371}$ with quotient 14.57

3. **(D)** $.4\overline{).64}$ with quotient 1.6

4. **(C)** $.12 \times \dfrac{2.0}{.5} = .12 \times 4 = .03$

5. **(D)** $\dfrac{10.20}{.03} \times \dfrac{1.7}{.1} = 340 \div 17 = 20$

Math Laws (Page 20)

1. **(D)** $8 + (4 \div 2) + (6 \cdot 3) - 1 = 8 + 2 + 18 - 1 = 27$
2. **(B)** $(16 \div 4) + (2 \cdot 3) + 2 - (8 \div 2) = 4 + 6 + 2 - 4 = 8$
3. **(C)**
4. **(E)**
5. **(D)**
6. **(A)**
7. **(B)**

Estimation (Page 22)

1. **(C)** Estimate $\dfrac{500 + 2000}{100} = \dfrac{2500}{100} = 25$, closest to 20

2. **(C)** Estimate $\dfrac{6000 \cdot 300}{400 + 600} = \dfrac{1,800,000}{1000} = 1800$

3. **(C)** Estimate $\dfrac{800 + 500}{1500 - 900} = \dfrac{1300}{600} =$ about 2

chapter **2**
Fractions

Important fractions in my life: awesome sale = $\frac{1}{2}$ price, slice of pizza = $\frac{1}{8}$ of the pie, time of school day spent in English class with hottie Holden next to me = $\frac{1}{10}$.

Simply put, fractions are *parts* of numbers. Fractions are used so often in daily life that you barely notice you're dealing in math terms. Common topics that use fractions are food, time, and money, like Chi explained above. In the pages that follow, you will learn how to add, subtract, multiply, divide, and simplify these guys.

31

Get Wise! Mastering Math Skills   *www.petersons.com*

ADDITION AND SUBTRACTION

To add fractions, they must have the same denominator (that's the number on the bottom, remember?). If there are only two fractions, we can use cross-multiplication:

Example: $\dfrac{4}{5} + \dfrac{7}{12}$

$$\dfrac{4}{5} \bowtie \dfrac{7}{12}$$

The easiest way to solve this addition problem is by cross-multiplication. If a birdie is on your shoulder screaming, "common denominators, common denominators," tell him to wait his turn. Finding a common denominator for the simple addition of two small fractions is a waste of time. Cross-multiplication is easier.

I've got a little birdie telling me that common denominators will be explained and used soon, so give your birdie a cracker and tell him to come back in 2 minutes.

So, to solve this, first multiply the cross products and add them on the top. Then multiply the two bottom numbers and place them on the bottom. It looks like this:

$$\frac{4(12) + 5(7)}{5(12)} = \frac{48 + 35}{60} = \frac{83}{60} = 1\frac{23}{60}$$

If there are more than two fractions, you have to find a common denominator. This is the smallest number that each denominator divides into neatly (no remainder).

Example: Add $\dfrac{1}{2}+\dfrac{1}{3}+\dfrac{1}{4}+\dfrac{1}{5}$.

Common denominators can be messy. Here's a cool trick: Pick out 5 (the biggest denominator number) and keep adding 5 to it until you get to a number that is divisible by all the rest of the denominators. By the way, these numbers (5, 10, 15, 20…) are called *multiples*. If done carefully, you'll stop at 60 and notice that 2, 3, and 4 also divide evenly into 60! That's your common denominator.

If you get stuck, you can multiply all the bottom numbers together. However, the numbers you'll end up with are going to be BIG. In this example, you'd get 120. Try the multiples trick above and you'll make fewer mistakes.

Back to the example: Once you have solved your common denominator dilemma, change each fraction so that the denominator is 60. You're really multiplying each fraction by a multiple of one:

If $\dfrac{30}{30}=1$ then you can multiply $\dfrac{1}{2}\cdot\dfrac{30}{30}=\dfrac{30}{60}$, and the fractions remain

equal. So $\dfrac{1}{2}=\dfrac{30}{60}$. Your new problem with new fraction equivalents looks like this:

$$\frac{30}{60}+\frac{20}{60}+\frac{15}{60}+\frac{12}{60}=\frac{77}{60}=1\frac{17}{60}$$

The numerators are added together to get 77 and this goes on top of your new common denominator of 60. You can simplify this to a mixed number if the answers are written in mixed form.

And here I was thinking that it's OK to believe that sometimes things in life just don't add up. Whatever.

34 . Fractions

Once you've figured out addition, subtraction is done the same way. Instead of adding the numerators, however, you must subtract them.

Example: $\dfrac{4}{5} - \dfrac{7}{12} = \dfrac{4(12) - 5(7)}{5(12)} = \dfrac{48 - 35}{60} = \dfrac{13}{60}$

Get Wise!

Try these problems and see if you've mastered the art of adding and subtracting fractions:

1. Find the sum of $\dfrac{1}{2} + \dfrac{2}{3} + \dfrac{3}{4}$.

   (A) $\dfrac{6}{9}$　　　　　(D) $\dfrac{6}{24}$

   (B) $\dfrac{23}{12}$　　　　(E) $2\dfrac{1}{3}$

   (C) $\dfrac{23}{36}$

2. Find the sum of $\dfrac{5}{17}$ and $\dfrac{3}{15}$.

   (A) $\dfrac{126}{255}$　　　(D) $\dfrac{40}{32}$

   (B) $\dfrac{40}{255}$　　　(E) $\dfrac{126}{265}$

   (C) $\dfrac{8}{32}$

3. From the sum of $\frac{3}{4}$ and $\frac{5}{6}$, subtract the sum of $\frac{1}{4}$ and $\frac{2}{3}$.

(A) 2

(D) $\frac{2}{3}$

(B) $\frac{1}{2}$

(E) $\frac{5}{24}$

(C) $\frac{36}{70}$

4. Subtract $\frac{3}{5}$ from $\frac{9}{11}$.

(A) $-\frac{12}{55}$

(D) $\frac{3}{8}$

(B) $\frac{12}{55}$

(E) $\frac{3}{4}$

(C) 1

5. Subtract $\frac{5}{8}$ from the sum of $\frac{1}{4}$ and $\frac{2}{3}$.

(A) 2

(D) $\frac{8}{15}$

(B) $\frac{3}{2}$

(E) $\frac{7}{24}$

(C) $\frac{11}{24}$

How wise? Check your answers on page 53.

MULTIPLICATION AND DIVISION

Multiplication of fractions is EASY! You just multiply across. Of course, you'll want to reduce them first or you'll end up with a number like $\dfrac{568920}{4321900}$, and that wouldn't be fun.

If I got an answer like $\dfrac{568920}{4321900}$, I'd *definitely* know something was off. I know math is tricky, but seriously, that wouldn't even fit in my calculator!

Example: $\dfrac{3}{5} \cdot \dfrac{15}{33} \cdot \dfrac{11}{45}$

You need to look at each number as a product of its factors. It's not difficult, just be aware that 15 is really 5×3, 33 is 11×3, and so on. Armed with this knowledge, you cancel out numbers that are found on both top and bottom! Remember, the more you can get rid of, the less you have to multiply in the end, so look carefully!

Interestingly, when you want to *divide* fractions, you need to multiply by the *multiplicative inverse*. Multiplicative inverse is just a fancy term for switching the top and bottom in the fraction you're dividing by.

Example: $\dfrac{5}{18} \div \dfrac{5}{9}$ is really saying $\dfrac{5}{18} \times \dfrac{9}{5}$. Cross out (cancel) the 5s and you're left with $\dfrac{9}{18}$ or $\dfrac{1}{2}$.

Get Wise!

Try these problems to see if you're a whiz at multiplying and dividing fractions:

1. Find the product of $\dfrac{3}{2}$, 6, $\dfrac{4}{9}$, and $\dfrac{1}{12}$.

    (A) 3

    (D) $\dfrac{1}{36}$

    (B) $\dfrac{1}{3}$

    (E) $\dfrac{5}{12}$

    (C) $\dfrac{14}{23}$

2. Find $\dfrac{7}{8} \cdot \dfrac{2}{3} \div \dfrac{1}{8}$.

    (A) $\dfrac{3}{14}$

    (D) $\dfrac{14}{3}$

    (B) $\dfrac{7}{96}$

    (E) $\dfrac{8}{3}$

    (C) $\dfrac{21}{128}$

3. $\dfrac{3}{5} \div \left(\dfrac{1}{2} \cdot \dfrac{3}{10} \right)$ is equal to

    (A) 4

    (D) $\dfrac{5}{12}$

    (B) $\dfrac{1}{4}$

    (E) $\dfrac{12}{15}$

    (C) $\dfrac{12}{5}$

4. Find $\dfrac{2}{3}$ of $\dfrac{7}{12}$.

   (A) $\dfrac{7}{8}$ (D) $\dfrac{8}{9}$

   (B) $\dfrac{7}{9}$ (E) $\dfrac{7}{18}$

   (C) $\dfrac{8}{7}$

5. Divide 5 by $\dfrac{5}{12}$.

   (A) $\dfrac{25}{12}$ (D) 12

   (B) $\dfrac{1}{12}$ (E) $\dfrac{12}{5}$

   (C) $\dfrac{5}{12}$

How wise? Check your answers on page 54.

KEEP IT SIMPLE

Simplicity is best. Sometimes tests and teachers require you to put your answers "in simplest form." Do not fear; the chart below will provide you with some tricks about factors that should make your life a whole lot easier.

★ Magic Factor Chart ★

If a number is divisible by	Then
2	its last digit is 0, 2, 4, 6, or 8
3	the sum of the digits is divisible by 3
4	the number formed by the last 2 digits is divisible by 4
5	the last digit is 5 or 0
6	the number meets the tests for divisibility by 2 and 3
8	the number formed by the last 3 digits is divisible by 8
9	the sum of the digits is divisible by 9

This chart works like magic, honest. Try it out!

Example: Find a number that will reduce $\dfrac{135,492}{428,376}$.

Since both numbers are even, they are at least divisible by 2. But we want to go for more.

The sum of the digits on the top is 24. The sum of the digits on the bottom is 30. Since these sums are both divisible by 3, both top and bottom are divisible by 3. Since these numbers meet the divisibility tests for 2 and 3, they are each divisible by 6.

These are more like solving a mystery than math. Let's try another one.

Example: Simplify $\dfrac{43,672}{52,832}$ to simplest form.

Solution: Again, since both numbers are even, they are divisible by 2.

But you knew that. Dig deeper. The sum of the digits in the top number is 22. This isn't divisible by 3. Try more. The numbers formed by the last two digits of both top and bottom are divisible by 4. This means both numbers are divisible by 4!

But that's not all. The last three numbers in each is divisible by 8. That's quite a large number. Divide by 8 and you get $\dfrac{5459}{6604}$.

Now the top number is no longer divisible by 2. And we already know that neither is divisible by 3. At this point it looks like you've gone as far as you can go with this bag of tricks. It's unlikely anyone would expect you to divide it by a two-digit number.

That factor chart DOES work! Yes, more, more, give me more factors!

Get Wise!

See what you've learned about keeping fractions simple.

1. Which of the following numbers is divisible by 5 and 9?

    (A) 42,235   (D) 37,845

    (B) 34,325   (E) 53,290

    (C) 46,505

2. Given the number $83,21p$, in order for this number to be divisible by 3, 6, and 9, p must be

    (A) 4   (D) 0

    (B) 5   (E) 9

    (C) 6

3. If *n!* means $n(n-1)(n-2) \ldots (4)(3)(2)(1)$, so that $4! = (4)(3)(2)(1)$ = 24, then 19! is divisible by

    I. 17

    II. 54

    III. 100

    IV. 39

(A) I and II only   (D) I, II, III, and IV

(B) I only   (E) none of the above

(C) I and IV only

4. The fraction $\dfrac{432}{801}$ can be simplified by dividing the numerator and denominator by

(A) 2   (D) 8

(B) 4   (E) 9

(C) 6

5. The number 6,862,140 is divisible by

    I. 3

    II. 4

    III. 5

(A) I only   (D) I, II, and III

(B) I and III only   (E) III only

(C) II and III only

How wise? Check your answers on page 54.

MIXING IT UP

Mixed numbers are treated the same as any other fractions. To add or subtract, you simply need to find a common denominator. You can even borrow, if necessary, in the terms of the common denominator.

Example: $23\frac{1}{3} - 6\frac{2}{5}$

Solution: Obviously, you can't take $\frac{2}{5}$ from $\frac{1}{3}$. Your common denominator is 15. Unfortunately, $\frac{1}{3}$ turns into $\frac{5}{15}$ and $\frac{2}{5}$ turns into $\frac{6}{15}$ and you realize the second term in your subtraction problem is the bigger one: $23\frac{5}{15} - 6\frac{6}{15}$. Not good. We can't have negative numbers here. What you need to do in this case is borrow from the 23. You make it 22 and add the equivalent of 1 to the fraction: $\frac{5}{15} + \frac{15}{15}$.

The problem is then rewritten as:

$$22\frac{20}{15}$$
$$-6\frac{6}{15}$$

So your answer is $16\frac{14}{15}$. Try another.

Example: $17\frac{3}{4} + 43\frac{3}{5}$

Solution: First, give the fractions a common denominator:

$$17\frac{3}{4} = 17\frac{15}{20}$$

$$+43\frac{3}{5} = +43\frac{12}{20}$$

$$= 60\frac{27}{20}$$

Add the two fractions to get $60\frac{27}{20}$, which can then be changed to $61\frac{7}{20}$.

WISE NOTE

To multiply or divide mixed numbers, always make them into improper fractions first.

Example: Multiply $3\frac{3}{5} \times 1\frac{1}{9} \times 2\frac{3}{4}$.

Solution: $\dfrac{18}{5} \times \dfrac{10}{9} \times \dfrac{11}{4} = \dfrac{\overset{2}{\cancel{18}}}{\cancel{5}_1} \times \dfrac{\overset{2}{\cancel{10}}}{\cancel{9}_1} \times \dfrac{11}{\cancel{4}_2} = 11$

Got it? Now try dividing.

Example: Divide $3\frac{3}{4}$ by $5\frac{5}{8}$.

Solution: $\dfrac{15}{4} \div \dfrac{45}{8} = \dfrac{15}{4} \times \dfrac{8}{45} = \dfrac{\overset{1}{\cancel{15}}}{\cancel{4}_1} \times \dfrac{\overset{2}{\cancel{8}}}{\cancel{45}_3} = \dfrac{2}{3}$

Get Wise!

That's all there is to it. Try these:

1. Find the sum of $1\frac{1}{16}, 2\frac{2}{3},$ and $3\frac{3}{4}$.

    (A) $7\frac{5}{12}$ (D) $6\frac{1}{3}$

    (B) $6\frac{6}{13}$ (E) $7\frac{1}{12}$

    (C) $7\frac{7}{12}$

2. Subtract $45\frac{5}{12}$ from 61.

    (A) $15\frac{7}{12}$ (D) $16\frac{5}{12}$

    (B) $15\frac{5}{12}$ (E) $17\frac{5}{12}$

    (C) $16\frac{7}{12}$

3. Find the product of $32\frac{1}{2}$ and $5\frac{1}{5}$.

    (A) 26   (D) $160\frac{1}{10}$

    (B) 13   (E) $160\frac{2}{7}$

    (C) 169

4. Divide $17\frac{1}{2}$ by 70.

(A) $\frac{1}{4}$ (D) $4\frac{1}{2}$

(B) 4   (E) $\frac{4}{9}$

(C) $\frac{1}{2}$

5. Find $1\frac{3}{4} \cdot 12 \div 8\frac{2}{5}$.

(A) $\frac{2}{5}$ (D) $\frac{1}{2}$

(B) $\frac{5}{288}$ (E) $2\frac{1}{2}$

(C) $2\frac{1}{5}$

How wise? Check your answers on page 55.

COMPARISON SHOPPING

The easiest way to compare fractions is to cross-multiply. Put the product (that's what you get when you multiply numbers, remember?) above the top of each side. Look:

Example: Compare $\frac{5}{6}$ to $\frac{8}{11}$.

This cross-multiplication comparing is cake! 55 is bigger than 48—even my little brother knows that and he still watches "Rugrats."

Solution: First, cross-multiply: $\dfrac{5}{6}^{55}$ $\dfrac{8}{11}^{48}$. Clearly, the bigger number is 55. Therefore, since it goes above the first number, $\dfrac{5}{6}$ is the bigger number.

It won't always be that easy, however. If more than one fraction is being compared, you may have to cross-multiply several times, or you can find a common denominator.

Example: Which of the following fractions is the largest?

(A) $\dfrac{3}{5}$ (D) $\dfrac{55}{64}$

(B) $\dfrac{21}{32}$ (E) $\dfrac{7}{8}$

(C) $\dfrac{11}{16}$

Solution: To compare the last four answer choices, use a common denominator of 64. This is what it looks like:

$$\frac{21}{32} = \frac{42}{64}; \frac{11}{16} = \frac{44}{64}; \frac{55}{64}; \frac{7}{8} = \frac{56}{64}$$

Clearly, $\dfrac{7}{8}$ is the largest of those four. Now cross-multiply $\dfrac{7}{8}$ and $\dfrac{3}{5}$, and you'll see that 35 is greater than 24, so $\dfrac{7}{8}$ is the biggest fraction.

Get Wise!

Try these five problems to see if you can compare with the best of them.

1. Arrange these fractions in order of size, from largest to smallest:

    $\frac{4}{15}, \frac{2}{5}, \frac{1}{3}$.

    (A) $\frac{4}{15}, \frac{2}{5}, \frac{1}{3}$ (D) $\frac{1}{3}, \frac{4}{15}, \frac{2}{5}$

    (B) $\frac{4}{15}, \frac{1}{3}, \frac{2}{5}$ (E) $\frac{1}{3}, \frac{2}{5}, \frac{4}{15}$

    (C) $\frac{2}{5}, \frac{1}{3}, \frac{4}{15}$

2. Which of the following fractions is the smallest?

    (A) $\frac{3}{4}$ (D) $\frac{19}{24}$

    (B) $\frac{5}{6}$ (E) $\frac{13}{15}$

    (C) $\frac{7}{8}$

3. Which of the following fractions is the largest?

    (A) $\frac{3}{5}$ (D) $\frac{3}{4}$

    (B) $\frac{7}{10}$ (E) $\frac{13}{20}$

    (C) $\frac{5}{8}$

4. Which of the following fractions is closest to $\dfrac{3}{4}$?

(A) $\dfrac{1}{2}$ (D) $\dfrac{11}{12}$

(B) $\dfrac{7}{12}$ (E) $\dfrac{19}{24}$

(C) $\dfrac{5}{6}$

5. Which of the following fractions is closest to $\dfrac{1}{2}$?

(A) $\dfrac{5}{12}$ (D) $\dfrac{31}{60}$

(B) $\dfrac{8}{15}$ (E) $\dfrac{7}{15}$

(C) $\dfrac{11}{20}$

How wise? Check your answers on page 56.

COMPLEXITY IS COMPLEX

"Never make anything simple and efficient when a way can be found to make it complex and wonderful."

—Unknown

Complexity facts I know: Pasta is full of complex carbohydrates, my best friend lives in a housing complex, and my mom says my aunt has a personality complex. Apparently, complexity is everywhere. Hope it's not contagious.

A *complex fraction* is a fraction that contains a fraction. To simplify a complex fraction, you need to multiply every term by the smallest number that will clear all fractions in the numerator and denominator.

Example:

$$\dfrac{\dfrac{1}{6}+\dfrac{1}{4}}{\dfrac{1}{2}+\dfrac{1}{3}}$$

Solution: All four denominators will divide easily into 12. You must multiply all of the fractions by 12 to get rid of the fractions: $\dfrac{1}{6}\times12$ is 2, $\dfrac{1}{4}\times12$ is 3, $\dfrac{1}{2}\times12$ is 6, and $\dfrac{1}{3}\times12$ is 4. Your new problem now looks like this: $\dfrac{2+3}{6+4}=\dfrac{5}{10}=\dfrac{1}{2}$.

Try a subtraction problem.

Example:

$$\dfrac{\dfrac{3}{4}-\dfrac{2}{3}}{1+\dfrac{1}{2}}$$

Solution: Again, multiply all terms by 12. Don't forget about the 1.

$$\dfrac{9-8}{12+6}=\dfrac{1}{18}$$

Get Wise!

This is the last section for this chapter on fractions. Show yourself what you're made of with complex fractions.

1. Write as a fraction in simplest form: $\dfrac{\dfrac{2}{3}+\dfrac{1}{6}+\dfrac{1}{4}}{\dfrac{2}{3}-\dfrac{1}{2}}$

(A) $\dfrac{13}{2}$ (D) $\dfrac{4}{13}$

(B) $\dfrac{7}{2}$ (E) $\dfrac{49}{12}$

(C) $\dfrac{13}{4}$

2. Simplify: $\dfrac{\dfrac{5}{6}-\dfrac{2}{3}}{\dfrac{5}{12}-\dfrac{1}{6}}$

(A) $\dfrac{5}{12}$ (D) $\dfrac{1}{6}$

(B) $\dfrac{5}{6}$ (E) $\dfrac{7}{12}$

(C) $\dfrac{2}{3}$

3. Find the value of $\dfrac{\dfrac{1}{a}+\dfrac{1}{b}}{\dfrac{1}{ab}}$ when $a = 2$ and $b = 3$.

(A) $\dfrac{5}{6}$

(D) $1\dfrac{1}{5}$

(B) 5

(E) $2\dfrac{2}{5}$

(C) $4\dfrac{1}{6}$

4. Find the value of $\dfrac{\dfrac{1}{a}+\dfrac{1}{b}}{\dfrac{1}{ab}}$ when $a = \dfrac{1}{2}$ and $b = \dfrac{1}{3}$.

(A) $\dfrac{5}{6}$

(D) $1\dfrac{1}{5}$

(B) 5

(E) $2\dfrac{2}{5}$

(C) $4\dfrac{1}{6}$

5. Find the value of $\dfrac{2\dfrac{1}{3}}{5\dfrac{1}{2}+3\dfrac{1}{3}}$.

(A) $\dfrac{4}{17}$

(D) $\dfrac{12}{51}$

(B) $\dfrac{21}{25}$

(E) $\dfrac{14}{53}$

(C) $\dfrac{7}{6}$

How wise? Check your answers on page 57.

A Word to the Wise

Fractions: The Vocabulary

★ The *numerator* is the number on top of the fraction.

★ The *denominator* is the number on the bottom of the fraction.

★ A *mixed number* contains an integer and a fraction.

★ An *improper fraction* is larger on the top than on the bottom.

★ To find the *multiplicative inverse*, switch around the top and bottom numbers.

★ A *complex* number is a fraction containing fractions.

Fractions: The Rules

To *add or subtract* two simple fractions:

★ Cross-multiply and perform the function on top.

★ Multiply across the bottom. Simplify if necessary.

Addition or subtraction of *multiple fractions* may require *common denominators*:

★ Find the smallest integer the denominators divide into.

★ Multiply each numerator by the same number the denominator is multiplied by to get to the common denominator.

★ Perform addition or subtraction on top. Use common denominator as the denominator.

WISE POINTS

★ *Mixed numbers* must be changed into *improper fractions* in order to work with them.

★ To *multiply* fractions, cancel out factors on top and bottom. Multiply what's left.

★ To *divide* fractions, switch the second fraction to its multiplicative inverse and multiply.

★ Memorize the *Magic Factor Chart* for quicker fraction simplification.

★ To *compare* fractions, cross-multiply and write the numbers above the numerators. The larger product is found over the larger fraction.

★ To solve a *complex fraction*, multiply all fractions by the smallest term that all denominators divide into.

ANSWERS TO CHAPTER 2: PRACTICE EXERCISES

Addition and Subtraction (Page 34)

1. **(B)** Change all fractions to twelfths:

$$\frac{6}{12}+\frac{8}{12}+\frac{9}{12}=\frac{23}{12}$$

2. **(A)** Cross-multiply:

$$\frac{5(15)+17(3)}{17(15)}=\frac{75+51}{255}=\frac{126}{255}$$

3. **(D)**

$$\frac{3}{4}+\frac{5}{6}=\frac{18+20}{24}=\frac{38}{24}=\frac{19}{12}$$

$$\frac{1}{4}+\frac{2}{3}=\frac{3+8}{12}=\frac{11}{12}$$

$$\frac{19}{12}-\frac{11}{12}=\frac{8}{12}=\frac{2}{3}$$

4. **(B)**

$$\frac{9}{11}-\frac{3}{5}=\frac{45-33}{55}=\frac{12}{55}$$

5. **(E)** $\dfrac{1}{4}+\dfrac{2}{3}=\dfrac{3+8}{12}=\dfrac{11}{12}$

$$\dfrac{11}{12}-\dfrac{5}{8}=\dfrac{88-60}{96}=\dfrac{28}{96}=\dfrac{7}{24}$$

Multiplication and Division (Page 37)

1. **(B)**

$$\dfrac{\cancel{3}^{1}}{\cancel{2}_{1}}\cdot\dfrac{\cancel{6}^{\cancel{3}^{1}}}{1}\cdot\dfrac{\cancel{4}^{1}}{\cancel{9}\,\cancel{3}_{1}}\cdot\dfrac{1}{\cancel{12}_{3}}=\dfrac{1}{3}$$

3. **(A)**

$$\dfrac{3}{5}\div\dfrac{3}{20}=\dfrac{\cancel{3}^{1}}{\cancel{5}^{1}}\cdot\dfrac{\cancel{20}^{4}}{\cancel{3}^{1}}=4$$

2. **(D)** $\dfrac{7}{\cancel{8}_{1}}\cdot\dfrac{2}{3}\cdot\dfrac{\cancel{8}^{1}}{1}=\dfrac{14}{3}$

4. **(E)** $\dfrac{\cancel{2}^{1}}{3}\cdot\dfrac{7}{\cancel{12}_{6}}=\dfrac{7}{18}$

5. **(D)** $\dfrac{\cancel{8}^{1}}{1}\cdot\dfrac{12}{\cancel{8}_{1}}=12$

Keep It Simple (Page 40)

Here's where that chart on page 39 comes in handy—did you use it? I did, and I saved time and money since I didn't have to punch numbers in my calculator and ruin my new manicure.

1. **(D)** The sum of the digits must be divisible by 9. (Obviously, you can see that all answers are divisible by 5, so only 9 counts). $3 + 7 + 8 + 4 + 5 = 27$, which is divisible by 9.

2. **(A)** The sum of the digits must be divisible by 9, and the digit must be even. $8 + 3 + 2 + 1 = 14$. If you try (A), you see that $14 + 4 = 18$, ding ding.

3. **(D)** If you haven't seen this before, it's a factorial. Just a weird way of saying $(19)(18)(17)(16) \ldots (3)(2)(1)$. This is divisible by 17 (as well as by all the other numbers from 18 to 1, duh). It is also divisible by 54, since it contains factors of 9 and 6. It is divisible by 100, since it contains factors of 10, 5, and 2. It is divisible by 39, since it contains factors of 13 and 3. And you thought math was useless!

4. **(E)** The sum of the digits in both top and bottom are divisible by 9.

5. **(D)** The sum of the digits is 27, which is divisible by 3. The number formed by the last two digits is 40, which is divisible by 4. The number ends in 0 and is therefore divisible by 5. Elementary, my dear Watson.

Mixed Numbers (Page 44)

1. **(C)** Add:
$$1\frac{1}{6} = 1\frac{2}{12}$$
$$2\frac{2}{3} = 2\frac{8}{12}$$
$$3\frac{3}{4} = 3\frac{9}{12}$$
$$6\frac{19}{12} = 7\frac{7}{12}$$

2. **(A)**
$$61 = 60\frac{12}{12}$$
$$45\frac{5}{12} = -45\frac{5}{12}$$
$$15\frac{7}{12}$$

3. **(C)** $\dfrac{\cancel{65}^{13}}{\cancel{2}_{1}} \cdot \dfrac{\cancel{26}^{13}}{\cancel{5}_{1}} = 169$

4. **(A)** $17\dfrac{1}{2}\cdot 70 = \dfrac{35}{2} \div 70 = \dfrac{\overset{1}{\cancel{35}}}{2}\cdot\dfrac{1}{\cancel{70}_2} = \dfrac{1}{4}$

5. **(E)** $\dfrac{\overset{1}{\cancel{7}}}{\cancel{4}_1}\cdot\dfrac{\overset{3}{\cancel{12}}^1}{1}\cdot\dfrac{5}{\cancel{42}_{6\,2}} = \dfrac{5}{2} = 2\dfrac{1}{2}$

Comparisons (Page 47)

1. **(C)** $\dfrac{2}{5} = \dfrac{6}{15};\ \dfrac{1}{3} = \dfrac{5}{15}$

2. **(A)** To compare choices (A), (B), (C), and (D), use a common denominator of 24.

$$\dfrac{3}{4} = \dfrac{18}{24};\quad \dfrac{5}{6} = \dfrac{20}{24};\quad \dfrac{7}{8} = \dfrac{21}{24};\quad \dfrac{19}{24}$$

The smallest fraction there is $\dfrac{3}{4}$. Compare $\dfrac{3}{4}$ with $\dfrac{13}{15}$ by cross-multiplying and writing the numbers above the numerators.

$(3)(15) = 45$ is less than $(4)(13) = 52$, so $\dfrac{3}{4} < \dfrac{13}{15}$.

3. **(D)** To compare choices (A), (B), (D), and (E), use a common denominator of 20.

$$\dfrac{3}{5} = \dfrac{12}{20};\quad \dfrac{7}{10} = \dfrac{14}{20};\quad \dfrac{3}{4} = \dfrac{15}{20};\quad \dfrac{13}{20}$$

Unlike above, $\dfrac{3}{4}$ is the largest. Compare $\dfrac{3}{4}$ with $\dfrac{5}{8}$ by cross-multiplying and writing the numbers above the numerators.

$(3)(8) = 24$ is greater than $(4)(5) = 20$. Thus, $\dfrac{3}{4}$ wins.

4. **(E)** Use a common denominator of 24.

$$\frac{1}{2}=\frac{12}{24} \quad \frac{7}{12}=\frac{14}{24} \quad \frac{5}{6}=\frac{20}{24} \quad \frac{11}{12}=\frac{22}{24} \quad \frac{19}{24}$$

Since $\frac{3}{4}=\frac{18}{24}$, the answer closest to $\frac{3}{4}$ is (E), $\frac{19}{24}$.

5. **(D)** Use a common denominator of 60.

$$\frac{5}{12}=\frac{25}{60} \quad \frac{8}{15}=\frac{32}{60} \quad \frac{11}{20}=\frac{33}{60} \quad \frac{31}{60} \quad \frac{7}{15}=\frac{28}{60}$$

Since $\frac{1}{2}=\frac{30}{60}$, the answer closest to $\frac{1}{2}$ is (D), $\frac{31}{60}$.

Complex Fractions (Page 50)

1. **(A)** Multiply every term of the fraction by 12:

$$\frac{8+2+3}{8-6}=\frac{13}{2}$$

2. **(C)** Multiply every term of the fraction by 12:

$$\frac{10-8}{5-2}=\frac{2}{3}$$

3. **(B)** Multiply every term by 6:

$$\frac{\frac{1}{2}+\frac{1}{3}}{\frac{1}{6}}=\frac{3+2}{1}=5$$

4. **(A)** $\dfrac{1}{\frac{1}{2}} = 2;\quad \dfrac{1}{\frac{1}{3}} = 3;\quad \dfrac{1}{\frac{1}{6}} = 6$

$$\frac{2+3}{6} = \frac{5}{6}$$

5. **(E)** Multiply every term by 6: $\dfrac{\dfrac{7}{3}}{\dfrac{11}{2} + \dfrac{10}{3}} = \dfrac{14}{33+20} = \dfrac{14}{53}$

Congratulations, you finished fractions. You are $\dfrac{2}{10}$ of the way through this book. Now, go have some fun!

chapter 3

Fraction Problems with Words

UNDERSTANDING WORD PROBLEMS

In this chapter, you will learn how to solve word problems that have fraction functions. If you have successfully learned all the ideas in the previous chapter, then this is the next logical step. You'll have to combine your ability to understand what the problem asks for with your knowledge of fractions. After the example(s) there will be a set of practice problems to see if you have the hang of the math that's involved.

> *Example:* Andrea and Danny ran for president of the junior class. Andrea got 15 votes, while Danny got the other 10. What fractional part of the votes did Andrea receive?

Solution: The first step here is to figure out the total number of votes. That's 25. Then you create a fraction with Andrea's total on the top: $\frac{15}{25}$ or $\frac{3}{5}$.

Get Wise!

Try the eight problems below to see if you understand this concept.

1. There are 18 boys and 12 girls in a class. What part of the class is girls?

   (A) $\frac{2}{3}$ (D) $\frac{1}{15}$

   (B) $\frac{3}{5}$ (E) $\frac{3}{2}$

   (C) $\frac{2}{5}$

2. A team played 40 games and lost 6. What part of the games played did the team win?

   (A) $\frac{3}{20}$ (D) $\frac{17}{20}$

   (B) $\frac{3}{17}$ (E) $\frac{7}{8}$

   (C) $\frac{14}{17}$

3. What part of an hour occurs between 3:45 p.m. and 4:09 p.m.?

   (A) $\dfrac{6}{25}$ (D) $\dfrac{1}{24}$

   (B) $\dfrac{2}{5}$ (E) 24

   (C) $\dfrac{5}{12}$

4. A camp employs 4 men, 6 women, 12 girls, and 8 boys. In the middle of the summer, 3 girls are fired and replaced by women. What part of the staff is then made up of women?

   (A) $\dfrac{1}{5}$ (D) $\dfrac{3}{10}$

   (B) $\dfrac{2}{9}$ (E) $\dfrac{1}{2}$

   (C) $\dfrac{1}{3}$

5. There are three times as many seniors as juniors at a high school dance. What part of the students present are juniors?

   (A) $\dfrac{2}{5}$ (D) $\dfrac{3}{4}$

   (B) $\dfrac{3}{5}$ (E) $\dfrac{1}{4}$

   (C) $\dfrac{2}{3}$

6. What part of a yard is 1 ft. 3 in.? (A yard is 3 ft.; a ft. is 12 in.)

   (A) $\dfrac{5}{12}$ (D) $\dfrac{5}{8}$

   (B) $\dfrac{1}{3}$ (E) $\dfrac{4}{9}$

   (C) $\dfrac{1}{2}$

7. Manorville High had a meeting of the Student Senate, which was attended by 10 freshmen, 8 sophomores, 15 juniors, and 7 seniors. What part of the students present at the meeting were sophomores?

   (A) $\dfrac{1}{4}$ (D) $\dfrac{1}{5}$

   (B) $\dfrac{5}{8}$ (E) $\dfrac{1}{3}$

   (C) $\dfrac{7}{40}$

8. The Dobkin family budgets its monthly income as follows: $\dfrac{1}{3}$ for food, $\dfrac{1}{4}$ for rent, $\dfrac{1}{10}$ for clothing, and $\dfrac{1}{5}$ for savings. What part is left for other expenses?

   (A) $\dfrac{3}{7}$ (D) $\dfrac{2}{15}$

   (B) $\dfrac{1}{6}$ (E) $\dfrac{3}{20}$

   (C) $\dfrac{7}{60}$

Only $\frac{1}{10}$ for clothes!? I sure hope those Dobkins from page 62 have one kid, or that's totally unfair!

How wise? Check your answers on page 73.

FRACTIONS OF FRACTIONS

Sometimes problems ask for a fractional part of a fraction, like $\frac{3}{5}$ of $\frac{2}{3}$. This really just asks you to multiply the fractions together: $\frac{3}{4}$ of $\frac{2}{3}$ is $\frac{1}{2}$.

    Example: One fourth of the employees at the Brown & Brown factory earn over $20,000 per year. One half of the remainder of employees earn between $15,000 and $20,000. What part of the employees earn less than $15,000 per year?

    Solution: You know one fourth, or $\frac{1}{4}$ earn over $20,000, and $\frac{1}{2}$ of the rest (which is $\frac{1}{2}$ of $\frac{3}{4}$ or $\frac{3}{8}$) earn between $15,000 and $20,000. Now you've figured out what $\frac{1}{4} + \frac{3}{8}$ or $\frac{5}{8}$ of the employees' salaries are. That leaves you with $\frac{3}{8}$ who must earn less than $15,000 per year.

    These types of problems require you to do them step by step. Organization is key. Let's go through another one.

Lovely, more organization. Organization is important in your closet or entertainment center, but in math? Who knew?

Example: A full bottle of formaldehyde is left open in the anatomy lab. If $\frac{1}{3}$ of the liquid evaporates in the first 12 hours and $\frac{2}{3}$ of the remainder evaporates in the second 12 hours, what part of the bottle is full at the end of 24 hours?

Solution: First, draw a picture:

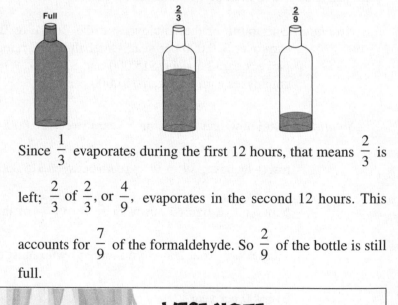

Since $\frac{1}{3}$ evaporates during the first 12 hours, that means $\frac{2}{3}$ is left; $\frac{2}{3}$ of $\frac{2}{3}$, or $\frac{4}{9}$, evaporates in the second 12 hours. This accounts for $\frac{7}{9}$ of the formaldehyde. So $\frac{2}{9}$ of the bottle is still full.

WISE NOTE

Drawing a picture will help you organize your information in many fraction problems.

Get Wise!

Try the problems below:

1. Mrs. Natt spent $\frac{2}{3}$ of the family income one year and divided the remainder among 4 different savings banks. If she put $2000 into each bank, what was the amount of her family income that year?
    (A) $8000   (D) $32,000
    (B) $16,000   (E) $6000
    (C) $24,000

2. After selling $\frac{2}{5}$ of the suits in his shop before Christmas, Mr. Gross sold the remainder of the suits at the same price per suit after Christmas for $4500. What was the income from the entire stock?
    (A) $3000   (D) $2700
    (B) $7500   (E) $8000
    (C) $1800

3. Of this year's graduating seniors at South High, $\frac{9}{10}$ will be going to college. Of these, $\frac{4}{5}$ will go to four-year colleges, while the rest will be going to two-year colleges. What part of the class will be going to two-year colleges?

    (A) $\frac{9}{50}$ (D) $\frac{36}{50}$

    (B) $\frac{1}{5}$ (E) $\frac{4}{25}$

    (C) $\frac{4}{5}$

4. Sue and Judy drove from New York to San Francisco, a distance of 3000 miles. They covered $\frac{1}{10}$ of the distance the first day and $\frac{2}{9}$ of the remaining distance the second day. How many miles were left to drive?

    (A) 600   (D) 2100
    (B) 2000   (E) 2700
    (C) 2400

5. Eight hundred employees work for the Metropolitan Transportation Company. One fourth of these are college graduates, while $\frac{5}{6}$ of the remainder are high school graduates. What part of the employees never graduated from high school?

    (A) $\frac{1}{6}$ (D) $\frac{1}{12}$

    (B) $\frac{1}{8}$ (E) $\frac{3}{4}$

    (C) $\frac{7}{8}$

How wise? Check your answers on page 74.

TRANSLATING WORD PROBLEMS

Sometimes a problem will give you a fractional part of a number and you have to find the whole. The easiest way to solve these is to translate the words into math symbols and create an equation.

Example: Vinny buys a used car for $2400, which is $\frac{2}{5}$ of the original price. Find the original price.

Solution: In word problems, a trick to remember is that "of" means "times"—it calls for multiplication. So $\frac{2}{5}$ of some number, which we'll call x, is $2400. In word problems, "is" always means "equals." Thus, you have your math problem:

$$\frac{2}{5}x = 2400$$

$$2x = 12000$$

$$x = \$6000$$

WISE NOTE

In math problems:

★ "of" means to multiply;

★ "is" means equals;

★ "what" stands for a variable.

One more example of this should solidify your skill.

Example: The gas tank on Justin's car reads $\frac{1}{8}$ full. He asks a gasoline attendant to fill the tank and finds that he needs 21 gallons. What is the full capacity of his tank?

Solution: Remember, "of" means "times," and "is" means "equals." Your equation looks like this:

$$21 = \frac{7}{8}x \qquad 168 = 7x \qquad 24 = x$$

Confused? Don't forget the other important math words like "please" and "help"! Don't worry—practice will make perfect.

Get Wise!
Work out the problems below and you'll be a whiz at the ideas above.

1. Daniel spent $4.50 for a ticket to the movies. This represents $\frac{3}{4}$ of his allowance for the week. What did he have left that week for other expenses?
   (A) $6.00
   (B) $4.00
   (C) $3.39
   (D) $1.13
   (E) $1.50

2. This year, 350 seniors attended the prom. This represents $\frac{7}{9}$ of the class. How many seniors did not attend the prom?
   (A) 50
   (B) 100
   (C) 110
   (D) 120
   (E) 450

3. A resolution was passed by a ratio of 5:4. If 900 people voted for the resolution, how many voted against it?
   (A) 500
   (B) 400
   (C) 720
   (D) 600
   (E) 223

4. Mr. Rich owns $\frac{2}{7}$ of a piece of property. If the value of his share is $14,000, what is the total value of the property?
   (A) $70,000
   (B) $49,000
   (C) $98,000
   (D) $10,000
   (E) $35,000

5.   The Stone family spends $500 per month for rent. This is $\frac{4}{15}$ of their total monthly income. Assuming that salaries remain constant, what is the Stone family income for one year?

   (A) $1875   (D) $22,500
   (B) $6000   (E) $16,000
   (C) $60,000

How wise? Check your answers on page 75.

INTRODUCING VARIABLES

Sometimes math problems will be written with letters in place of numbers. Just treat the letters as numbers and apply the same rules.

Example 1: It takes Mr. Simpson X days to paint his house. If he works for D days, what part of his house must still be painted?

Solution: Since you know that if the problem had given you numbers, say that he worked for 2 days and it takes him 5 days to paint his house, you would subtract 2 from 5 to figure out how many days of painting were left for Mr. Simpson. This number would then be the top number of a fraction with the total number of days, 5, on the bottom. But there are no numbers, so you must use X and D instead. Your answer is $\frac{X-D}{X}$.

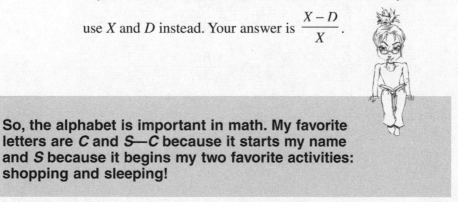

So, the alphabet is important in math. My favorite letters are *C* and *S*—*C* because it starts my name and *S* because it begins my two favorite activities: shopping and sleeping!

Example 2: Sue buys 500 stamps for her grandmother. X of these are 10-cent stamps, while $\frac{1}{3}$ of the remainder are 15-cent stamps. How many 15-cent stamps did Sue buy?

Solution: The amount of stamps Sue bought that *weren't* 10-cent stamps

is $(500 - X)$. This is treated as a regular number. We know $\frac{1}{3}$ of

that number are 15-cent stamps. There's your equation:

$\frac{1}{3}(500 - X)$ or $\frac{500 - X}{3}$.

Example 3: Joe spent $X on the latest U2 CD. This was $\frac{1}{M}$ of his weekly

allowance. What is Joe's weekly allowance?

Solution: Translate the sentence into math: $X = \frac{1}{M} \cdot A$, where A is total

allowance. Multiply by M; Thus, $MX = A$.

Get Wise!

Work out the problems below involving variables.

1. A class contains B boys and G girls. What part of the class is boys?

(A) $\dfrac{B}{G}$ (D) $\dfrac{B+G}{B}$

(B) $\dfrac{G}{B}$ (E) $\dfrac{B}{B-G}$

(C) $\dfrac{B}{B+G}$

2. M men agreed to rent a ski lodge for a total of D dollars. By the time they signed the contract, the price had increased by $100. Find the amount each man had to contribute as his total share.

(A) $\dfrac{D}{M}$

(D) $\dfrac{M}{D}+100$

(B) $\dfrac{D}{M}+100$

(E) $\dfrac{M+100}{D}$

(C) $\dfrac{D+100}{M}$

3. Of S students in Bryant High, $\dfrac{1}{3}$ study French and $\dfrac{1}{4}$ of the remainder study Italian. How many of the students study Italian?

(A) $\dfrac{1}{6}S$

(D) $\dfrac{1}{12}S$

(B) $\dfrac{1}{4}S$

(E) $\dfrac{3}{7}S$

(C) $\dfrac{2}{3}S$

4. Mr. and Mrs. Feldman took t dollars in travelers checks with them on a trip. During the first week, they spent $\dfrac{1}{5}$ of their money. During the second week, they spent $\dfrac{1}{3}$ of the remainder. How much did they have left at the end of the second week?

(A) $\dfrac{4t}{15}$

(D) $\dfrac{11t}{15}$

(B) $\dfrac{t}{15}$

(E) $\dfrac{8t}{15}$

(C) $\dfrac{7t}{15}$

5. Frank's gas tank was $\frac{1}{4}$ full. After putting in G gallons of gasoline, the tank was $\frac{7}{8}$ full. What was the capacity of the tank?

(A) $\dfrac{5G}{8}$ (D) $\dfrac{7G}{8}$

(B) $\dfrac{8G}{5}$ (E) $4G$

(C) $\dfrac{8G}{7}$

How wise? Check your answers on page 76.

A Word to the Wise

Fractions and Word Problems: The Vocabulary

★ "of" means multiplication

★ "is" means equal

★ "what" means a variable

Fractions and Word Problems: The Facts

★ The *rule* to follow with word problems involving fractions is to remember a fraction is simply part of a whole, or $\dfrac{\text{part}}{\text{whole}}$.

★ Fraction word problems are often *long*. Do them *piece-by-piece,* and it will be easier.

★ Remember, if the answer you got isn't a choice, you might have to *reduce!*

ANSWERS TO CHAPTER 3: PRACTICE EXERCISES

Understanding Word Problems (Page 60)

1. **(C)** $\frac{12}{30}$ or $\frac{2}{5}$ of the class is made up of girls.

2. **(D)**   The team won $\frac{34}{40}$, or $\frac{17}{20}$ of its games. Go team!

3. **(B)**   24 minutes is $\frac{24}{60}$ or $\frac{2}{5}$ of an hour, which is about as long as it could take you to forget all this.

4. **(D)**   The number of staff members stayed the same, they just got hit by child labor laws. Of these 30, 9 are now women. Therefore, $\frac{9}{30}$ or $\frac{3}{10}$ of the staff are women.

5. **(E)**   Let x = the number of juniors at the dance. $3x$ = the number of seniors at the dance. Then $4x$ = the number of students at the dance. x out of these $4x$ are juniors. That's $\frac{x}{4x}$ or $\frac{1}{4}$. See? Algebra can be fun.

6. **(A)**   Bet you didn't get it right if you forgot to change all measurements to inches. $\frac{15}{36} = \frac{5}{12}$

7. **(D)**   There were 40 students at the meeting. $\frac{8}{40} = \frac{1}{5}$

8. **(C)** $\frac{1}{3} + \frac{1}{4} + \frac{1}{10} + \frac{1}{5} = \frac{20}{60} + \frac{15}{60} + \frac{6}{60} + \frac{12}{60} = \frac{53}{60}$ Due to poor budgeting, only $\frac{7}{60}$ is left for other expenses.

Fractions of Fractions (Page 65)

1. **(C)** She put $8000 into savings banks.

    $$8000 = \frac{1}{3}x \quad \text{(Multiply by 3.)}$$
    $$\$24,000 = x$$

2. **(B)** Did you forget the problem asked for the ENTIRE profit? Take it step-by-step to avoid these novice errors. Three fifths were sold for $4500. So each fifth cost $1500, after the holidays no less. Mr. Gross is a lucky man! $1500 \times 5 = \$7500$.

3. **(A)** In this special town of brainiacs we must keep in mind that $\frac{4}{5}$ of $\frac{9}{10}$ will go to four-year colleges. So $\frac{1}{5}$ of $\frac{9}{10}$, or $\frac{9}{50}$, (multiplication, remember?) will go to two-year colleges.

4. **(D)** They covered only $\frac{1}{10} \cdot 3000$ or 300 miles the first day. This leaves 2700 miles still to drive. (Hope they have a CD player.) They covered $\frac{2}{9} \cdot 2700$ or 600 miles the second day, leaving 2100 miles still to drive. We'd suggest a faster pace.

Faster pace? I'll say. (yawn) At that rate, their cross-country drive will take longer than it took my history teacher to cover all of the Western Expansion!

5. **(B)** First find out who's not a learned college grad: $\frac{3}{4}$. And $\frac{5}{6}$ of $\frac{3}{4}$ or $\frac{5}{8}$ are high school graduates. Since $\frac{1}{4}$ are college graduates, and at

least $\dfrac{5}{8}$ finished twelfth grade, then $\dfrac{1}{4} + \dfrac{5}{8} = \dfrac{2}{8} + \dfrac{5}{8} = \dfrac{7}{8}$ of the

employees graduated from high school, leaving $\dfrac{1}{8}$ who did not.

Remember to find a common denominator before adding fractions! (We're to assume here that one cannot complete college without first finishing high school. We hope that didn't strain your brain too much).

Translating Word Problems (Page 68)

1. **(E)** $4.50 = \dfrac{3}{4}x$ (Multiply by 4.)

   $18.00 = 3x$ (Divide by 3.)

   $6.00 = x$

Thus, $x = \$6.00$, his allowance for the week. $\$6.00 - \$4.50 = \$1.50$ left for other expenses. Ooh, now he can get that car he always wanted.

2. **(B)** $350 = \dfrac{7}{9}x$ (Multiply by 9.)

   $3150 = 7x$ (Divide by 7.)

   $450 = x$

This is the number of students in the class. If 350 attend the prom, $450 - 350 = 100$ do not. And don't assume it's because they're ugly, reclusive, and have faces like Attack of the Monster Zit II.

3. **(C)** $\dfrac{5}{9}$ of the voters voted for the resolution.

$$900 = \dfrac{5}{9}x \quad \text{(Multiply by 9.)}$$

$$8100 = 5x \quad \text{(Divide by 5.)}$$

$$1620 = x$$

1620 – 900 = 720 voted against the resolution. By the way, what the heck is a resolution?

4.   **(B)** $\dfrac{2}{7}x = 14,000$ (Multiply by 7.)

$2x = 98,000$ (Divide by 2.)

$x = \$49,000$

5.   **(D)** $\dfrac{4}{15}x = 500$ (Multiply by 15.)

$4x = 7500$ (Divide by 4.)

$x = \$1875$ (This is their *monthly* income.)

Now, you can surely figure out to multiply by 12 to find yearly income: $22,500.

Introducing Variables (Page 70)

1.   **(C)**   There are $B + G$ students in the class. B out of $B + G$ are boys.

2.   **(C)**   The total cost is $D + 100$. Divide this by the number of men to find each share.

3.   **(A)** $\dfrac{1}{3}S$ students study French. $\dfrac{1}{4}$ of $\dfrac{2}{3}S$, or $\dfrac{1}{6}S$, study Italian. And they are the lucky ones.

4.   **(E)**   They spent $\dfrac{1}{5}t$ the first week. They spent $\dfrac{1}{3}$ of $\dfrac{4}{5}t$ or $\dfrac{4}{15}t$ the second week. During these two weeks they spent a total of $\dfrac{1}{5}t + \dfrac{4}{15}t$ or $\dfrac{7}{15}t$, leaving $\dfrac{8}{15}t$. Now, get rid of your t and go find some real money.

5.   **(B)** G gallons will fill $\dfrac{7}{8} - \dfrac{1}{4}$, or $\dfrac{5}{8}$, of the tank. $\dfrac{5}{8}x = G$

To solve for x, multiply by $\dfrac{8}{5}$: $x = \dfrac{8G}{5}$

May your gas tank always be full! Go have a study break!

chapter 4
Ratios and Proportions

RATIOS

I know ratios. For example, the ratio of people awake to people asleep during tenth period is always 1:5.

A *ratio* is a comparison. To write a ratio, you must remember to use the same unit.

Get Wise! Mastering Math Skills   *www.petersons.com*

Example 1: Express the ratio of 1 hour to 1 day.

Solution: You cannot write a ratio using both hours and days as units. You must first convert days to hours. One day is the same as 24 hours. So, the ratio for 1 hour to 1 day (24 hours) would be written as 1:24.

Example 2: Find the ratio of the shaded portion to the unshaded portion.

Solution: Since 5 of 9 squares are shaded, the ratio of shaded to unshaded is 5:4.

PROPORTIONS

A *proportion* is when you equate two ratios. Think of two sides of a scale that are equally balanced. Basically, you're setting two fractions equal and cross-multiplying to solve for whatever unknown quantity you have.

Example 1: Solve for x: $\dfrac{x+3}{5} = \dfrac{8-x}{6}$

Solution: Cross-multiply and solve for x: $6x + 18 = 40 - 5x$

$$11x = 22$$
$$x = 2$$

Example 2: Solve for x in $4{:}x = 9{:}18$

Solution: Rewrite the ratio in fraction form: $\dfrac{4}{x} = \dfrac{9}{18}$

Then cross-multiply: $9x = 72$. So $x = 8$.

Proportions can be done more quickly if you can see patterns. If your brain immediately detected that the second fraction in the above example is equal to $\frac{1}{2}$, then you can just say to yourself, *4 is one half of what?* 4 is half of 8!

Get Wise!

Try the following ratio and proportion problems.

1. Find the ratio of 1 ft. 4 in. to 1 yd.
    (A) 1:3   (D) 3:5
    (B) 2:9   (E) 5:12
    (C) 4:9

2. A team won 25 games in a 40-game season. Find the ratio of games won to games lost.

    (A) $\frac{5}{8}$ (D) $\frac{5}{3}$

    (B) $\frac{3}{8}$ (E) $\frac{3}{2}$

    (C) $\frac{3}{5}$

3. In the proportion $a:b = c:d$, solve for d in terms of a, b, and c.

    (A) $\frac{ac}{b}$ (D) $\frac{a}{bc}$

    (B) $\frac{bc}{a}$ (E) $\frac{bc}{d}$

    (C) $\frac{ab}{c}$

4. Solve for x: $\dfrac{x+1}{8} = \dfrac{28}{32}$

(A) $6\dfrac{1}{2}$ (D) 7

(B) 5   (E) 6

(C) 4

5. Solve for y: $\dfrac{2y}{9} = \dfrac{y-1}{3}$

(A) 3   (D) $\dfrac{9}{4}$

(B) $\dfrac{1}{3}$ (E) $\dfrac{4}{9}$

(C) $\dfrac{9}{15}$

How wise? Check your answers on page 87.

VARIETY IN PROPORTION

Sometimes a math problem tells you that quantities get bigger or smaller in the same direction. We call these *direct proportions*. Just make sure you keep the units the same on both sides of the equal sign when solving direct proportions problems.

> *Example 1:* If 4 bottles of milk cost $2, how many bottles can you buy for $8?

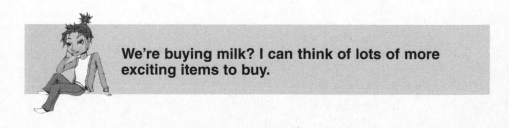

We're buying milk? I can think of lots of more exciting items to buy.

Solution: Keep the number of bottles on top and the cost on the bottom and replace what you don't know with x: $\frac{4}{2} = \frac{x}{8}$. Cross-multiply and you get $2x = 32$ or $x = 16$.

By the way, were you able to figure out the shortcut on the problem above? If so, you'd have seen that 4 is twice 2 and 16 is twice 8. Keep it in proportion!

Example 2: If b boys can deliver n pizzas in one hour, how many pizzas can c boys deliver in the same amount of time?

Solution: There is no real number answer here, only variables. Just remember to keep the same units on top and bottom: $\frac{b}{n} = \frac{c}{x}$.

To solve for x, cross-multiply: $bx = cn$

$$x = \frac{cn}{b}$$

Get Wise!

Try your luck at the proportions below.

1. Find the cost, in cents, of 8 books if 3 books of the same kind cost D dollars.

   (A) $\dfrac{8D}{3}$

   (B) $\dfrac{3}{800D}$

   (C) $\dfrac{3}{8D}$

   (D) $\dfrac{800D}{3}$

   (E) $\dfrac{108D}{3}$

2. On a map, $\frac{1}{2}$ inch = 10 miles. How many miles apart are two towns that are $2\frac{1}{4}$ inches apart on the map?

   (A) $11\frac{1}{4}$ (D) $40\frac{1}{2}$

   (B) 45   (E) 42

   (C) $22\frac{1}{2}$

3. The toll on the Intercoastal Thruway is 8¢ for every 5 miles traveled. What is the toll for a trip of 115 miles on this road?
   (A) $9.20   (D) $1.64
   (B) $1.70   (E) $1.76
   (C) $1.84

4. Mark's car uses 20 gallons of gas to drive 425 miles. At this rate, approximately how many gallons of gas will he need for a trip of 1000 miles?
   (A) 44   (D) 47
   (B) 45   (E) 49
   (C) 46

5. If r planes can carry p passengers, how many planes are needed to carry m passengers?

   (A) $\dfrac{rm}{p}$ (D) $\dfrac{pm}{r}$

   (B) $\dfrac{rp}{m}$ (E) $\dfrac{m}{rp}$

   (C) $\dfrac{p}{rm}$

How wise? Check your answers on page 88.

VARIETY IS THE SPICE OF LIFE

The proportions you solved above varied in the same direction. The next ones you'll see are *inverse*, which means that they vary in opposite directions. Some common examples of this inverse relationship are:

★ The bigger a diameter of a wheel, the smaller number of revolutions per minute

★ The more people hired to do a job, the less time it will take to do the job

★ The greater a demand for a commodity, like video game consoles during the holidays, the less time that commodity will last

Luckily for mathematicians, the *product* of the two relationships will remain constant. Watch this:

Example: If 3 men can paint a house in 2 days, how long will it take 2 men to do the job?

Solution: This is an inverse relationship. The fewer men, the more days it will take to paint the house:

$$\frac{3}{2} = \frac{2}{x}$$
$$3 \cdot x = 2 \cdot 2$$
$$3x = 4$$
$$x = \frac{4}{3} = 1\frac{1}{3} \text{ days}$$

Get Wise!

Work out the problems below on inverse relationships.

1. A field can be plowed by 8 machines in 6 hours. If 5 machines are broken and cannot be used, how many hours will it take to plow the field?

(A) 12

(B) $9\frac{3}{5}$

(C) $3\frac{3}{4}$

(D) 4

(E) 16

2. Camp Starlight has enough milk to feed 90 children for 4 days. If 10 of the children do not drink milk, how many days will the supply last?

   (A) 5

   (B) 6

   (C) $4\dfrac{1}{2}$

   (D) $4\dfrac{1}{8}$

   (E) $5\dfrac{1}{3}$

3. A pulley revolving at 200 revolutions per minute has a diameter of 15 inches. It is belted to a second pulley, which revolves at 150 revolutions per minute. Find the diameter, in inches, of the second pulley.

   (A) 11.2

   (B) 20

   (C) 18

   (D) 16.4

   (E) 2

4. Two boys weighing 60 pounds and 80 pounds balance a seesaw. How many feet from the fulcrum must the heavier boy sit if the lighter boy is 8 feet from the fulcrum?

   (A) 10

   (B) $10\dfrac{2}{3}$

   (C) 9

   (D) $7\dfrac{1}{2}$

   (E) 6

5. A gear with 20 teeth revolving at 200 revolutions per minute is meshed with a second gear turning at 250 revolutions per minute. How many teeth does this gear have?

   (A) 16

   (B) 25

   (C) 15

   (D) 10

   (E) 24

How wise? Check your answers on page 89.

So proportions can vary directly or inversely. Sounds easy
enough. Teenagers are always worried about their
proportions. But it seems to me that it is always one of those
direct variations—the more we eat, the bigger we get!

Get Wise!

Got it? Great, then you're ready. The problems below are either direct
proportions or inverse proportions. YOU decide. Good luck!

1. A farmer has enough chicken feed to last 30 chickens for 4 days. If
    10 more chickens are added, how many days will the feed last?

    (A) 3

    (B) $1\frac{1}{3}$

    (C) 12

    (D) $2\frac{2}{3}$

    (E) $5\frac{1}{3}$

2. At c cents per can, what is the cost of p cases of soda if there are 12
    cans in a case?

    (A) $12cp$

    (B) $\frac{cp}{12}$

    (C) $\frac{12}{cp}$

    (D) $\frac{12p}{c}$

    (E) $\frac{12c}{p}$

3. If m boys can put up a fence in d days, how many days will it take to put up the fence if two of the boys cannot participate?

    (A) $\dfrac{d}{-2}$ (D) $\dfrac{m-2}{md}$

    (B) $\dfrac{d(m-2)}{m}$ (E) $\dfrac{m(m-2)}{d}$

    (C) $\dfrac{md}{m-2}$

4. A recipe calls for $\dfrac{3}{4}$ lb. of butter and 18 oz. of sugar. If only 10 oz. of butter are available, how many ounces of sugar should be used?

    (A) $13\dfrac{1}{2}$ (D) 14

    (B) 23   (E) 15

    (C) 24

5. If 3 kilometers are equal to 1.8 miles, how many kilometers are equal to 100 miles?

    (A) 60   (D) $150\dfrac{1}{2}$

    (B) $166\dfrac{2}{3}$ (E) 160.4

    (C) 540

How wise? Check your answers on page 90.

A Word to the Wise

Ratios: The Facts

★ A *ratio* is a *comparison*.

★ Keep *units the same*.

★ Write as a *fraction* or with a *colon*.

Proportions: The Facts

★ A *proportion* is two ratios set equal.

★ They may be *direct or inverse*.

★ They are solved by *cross-multiplication*.

ANSWERS TO CHAPTER 4: PRACTICE EXERCISES

Ratios and Proportions (Page 79)

   1. **(C)** 1 ft. 4 in. = 16 in.

               1 yd. = 36 in.

$$\frac{16}{36} = \frac{4}{9}$$

   2. **(D)** They won 25 games and lost 15: $\frac{25}{15} = \frac{5}{3}$

   3. **(B)** $\frac{a}{b} = \frac{c}{d}$ (Cross-multiply.)

          $ad = bc$ (Divide by a.)

$$d = \frac{bc}{a}$$

4. **(E)** $32(x+1) = 28(8)$

$$32x + 32 = 224$$
$$32x = 192$$
$$x = 6$$

5. **(A)** $9(y-1) = 2y(3)$

$$9y - 9 = 6y$$
$$3y = 9$$
$$y = 3$$

It's all about cross-multiplying. Hope you figured it out!

Direct Variety (Page 81)

1. **(D)**   You are comparing books with cents. Don't forget that D dollars is equivalent to $100D$ cents.

$$\frac{3}{100D} = \frac{8}{x}$$
$$3x = 800D$$
$$x = \frac{800D}{3}$$

2. **(B)**   You compare inches to miles:

$$\frac{\frac{1}{2}}{10} = \frac{2\frac{1}{4}}{x} \quad \text{(Cross-multiply.)}$$
$$\frac{1}{2}x = 22\frac{1}{2} \quad \text{(Multiply by 2.)}$$
$$x = 45$$

3.   **(C)**   You compare cents to miles:

$$\frac{8}{5} = \frac{x}{115} \quad \text{(Cross-multiply.)}$$
$$5x = 920$$
$$x = \$1.84$$

4.   **(D)**   You compare gallons to miles:

$$\frac{20}{425} = \frac{x}{1000} \quad \text{(Cross-multiply.)}$$
$$425x = 20,000 \quad \text{(Avoid large numbers!)}$$
$$17x = 800 \quad \text{(Divide by 25.)}$$
$$x = 47\frac{1}{17}$$

5.   **(A)**   You compare planes to passengers:

$$\frac{r}{p} = \frac{x}{m} \quad \text{(Cross-multiply.)}$$
$$px = rm \quad \text{(Divide by } p.)$$
$$x = \frac{rm}{p}$$

Inverse Variety (Page 83)

1.   **(B)**   The number of machines times the hours needed remains constant (that means they can be set equal—it's a proportion, right?).

$$8 \cdot 6 = 5 \cdot x$$
$$5x = 48$$
$$x = 9\frac{3}{5}$$

2. **(C)** The number of children times the days remains constant.

$$90 \cdot 4 = 80 \cdot x$$
$$80x = 360$$
$$x = 4\frac{1}{2}$$

3. **(B)** Diameter times speed remains constant.

$$15 \cdot 200 = x \cdot 150$$
$$3000 = 150x$$
$$x = 20$$

4. **(E)** Weight times distance from fulcrum remains constant.

$$80x = 60 \cdot 8$$
$$80x = 480$$
$$x = 6$$

5. **(A)** Number of teeth times speed remains constant.

$$20 \cdot 200 = x \cdot 250$$
$$250x = 4000$$
$$x = 16$$

Direct and Inverse Proportions (Page 85)

1. **(A)** The more chickens, the fewer days. This is *inverse*.

$$30 \cdot 4 = 40x$$
$$40x = 120$$
$$x = 3$$

2. **(A)** The more cases, the more cents. This is *direct*. You compare cents with cans. In p cases there will be $12p$ cans.

$$\frac{c}{1} = \frac{x}{12p}$$
$$x = 12cp$$

3. **(C)** The fewer boys, the more days. This is *inverse*.

$$m \cdot d = (m-2) \cdot x$$

$$\frac{md}{m-2} = x$$

4. **(E)** The less butter, the less sugar. This is *direct*. If you've taken home economics (why do they call it economics when you cook all day, anyway?), you'll know 16 ounces are in pound, so change $\frac{3}{4}$ pounds to 12 ounces first or you'll have one sick-tasting recipe.

$$\frac{12}{18} = \frac{10}{x}$$

$$12x = 180$$

$$x = 15$$

5. **(B)** The more kilometers, the more miles. This is *direct*.

$$\frac{3}{1.8} = \frac{x}{100}$$

$$1.8x = 300$$

$$18x = 3000$$

$$x = 166\frac{2}{3}$$

Whew! All done with those proportions. Now I can go work on making my fun proportionate to all this learning.

chapter 5

Percents

CONVERSIONS

When you're in English class, you'll often look at roots of words to figure out their meanings. You can do the same thing with some math words, like *percent*. In Spanish, *cien* means one hundred. In French, it's *cent*. Therefore, *percent* really means "per one-hundred." With that in mind, you can see that 5% means 5 per 100. One more step will lead us to the conversions.

The word *per* can also be represented by a (/) sign as in hours/week or $/hour. This can also be written as the bar of a fraction. Therefore, 5% or 5 per 100 is the same as 5/100, or $\frac{5}{100}$. As a decimal, this is written as .05. These are known as *conversions*.

93

Roots are helpful in my SAT vocab class. For example, I learned a great word for "without feeling" in the *Get Wise! Mastering Vocabulary* book: *apathy*. In some old language, the "a" meant "without" and "pathos" were "feelings." I guess this would be a good word to describe the numbness I used to feel after doing too many math word problems until I bought this book.

Here are some conversions:

3.4% means 3.4 per 100. As a fraction, this is $\frac{3.4}{100}$. As a decimal, this is .034.

$\frac{1}{4}$% means $\frac{1}{4}$ per 100. As a fraction, this is $\frac{\frac{1}{4}}{100}$. As a decimal, this is .0025.

Treat a variable the same way:

c% means c per 100. As a fraction, this is $\frac{c}{100}$. As a decimal, this is .01c.

To change a *percent* to a *decimal*: Move the decimal two places to the *left*. This is because we are really dividing by 100.

$$62\% = .62 \qquad .4\% = .004 \qquad 3.2\% = .032$$

To change a *decimal* to a *percent*: Move the decimal two places to the *right*. This is the same as multiplying by 100.

$$.27 = 27\% \qquad .012 = 1.2\% \qquad .003 = .3\%$$

To change a *percent* to a *fraction*: Take away the percent sign and divide by 100. This is because "percent" means "per 100," remember? You can simplify, too.

$$25\% = \frac{25}{100} = \frac{1}{4}$$

$$70\% = \frac{70}{100} = \frac{7}{10}$$

$$.5\% = \frac{.5}{100} = \frac{5}{1000} = \frac{1}{200}$$

To change a *fraction* to a *percent*: Do the opposite. Multiply by 100 and write the percent sign.

$$\frac{4}{5} = \frac{4}{\cancel{5}} \cdot \cancel{100}^{20} \% = 80\%$$

$$\frac{3}{8} = \frac{3}{\cancel{8}_2} \cdot \cancel{100}^{25} \% = \frac{75}{2}\% = 37\frac{1}{2}\%$$

Great, now I know how to change decimals, fractions, and percents into each other. How did I ever think I could go on without such knowledge?

If a fraction doesn't convert easily because the denominator doesn't go into 100, you can change the fraction to a decimal first. Fractions are easily converted to decimals by dividing the top by the bottom. Then change the decimal to a percent.

Example: $\quad \dfrac{8}{17} = 17\overline{)8.00}^{.47} = 47\frac{1}{17}\%$

$$\begin{array}{r} 68 \\ \hline 120 \\ 119 \\ \hline 1 \end{array}$$

Memory Lane

There are certain fraction and decimal equivalents that are so common that memorizing them now would save you a lot of time. Remember, time is of the essence on many standardized tests.

Also, think how cool you'll feel when you yell at someone for eating your pizza by saying, "Hey, that's 40 percent," instead of saying, "Hey, that was 2 out of 5 pieces."

★ Conversion Chart ★

PERCENT	DECIMAL	FRACTION
50%	.5	$\frac{1}{2}$
25%	.25	$\frac{1}{4}$
75%	.75	$\frac{3}{4}$
10%	.1	$\frac{1}{10}$
30%	.3	$\frac{3}{10}$
70%	.7	$\frac{7}{10}$
90%	.9	$\frac{9}{10}$

(continued)

★ Conversion Chart (continued) ★

PERCENT	DECIMAL	FRACTION
$33\frac{1}{3}\%$	$.3\overline{3}$	$\frac{1}{3}$
$66\frac{2}{3}\%$	$.6\overline{6}$	$\frac{2}{3}$
$16\frac{2}{3}\%$	$.1\overline{6}$	$\frac{1}{6}$
$83\frac{1}{3}\%$	$.8\overline{3}$	$\frac{5}{6}$
20%	$.2$	$\frac{1}{5}$
40%	$.4$	$\frac{2}{5}$
60%	$.6$	$\frac{3}{5}$
80%	$.8$	$\frac{4}{5}$
$12\frac{1}{2}\%$	$.125$	$\frac{1}{8}$
$37\frac{1}{2}\%$	$.375$	$\frac{3}{8}$
$62\frac{1}{2}\%$	$.625$	$\frac{5}{8}$
$87\frac{1}{2}\%$	$.875$	$\frac{7}{8}$

Get Wise!

Try the percent conversions below. Refer to the beginning of Chapter 5 if you need help. Understand that wrong answers are meant to trick you!

1. Write $3\frac{1}{2}\%$ as a decimal.

    (A) 3.5   (D) .0035
    (B) .35   (E) 3.05
    (C) .035

2. Write 85% as a fraction in simplest form.

    (A) $\frac{13}{20}$ (D) $\frac{19}{20}$

    (B) $\frac{17}{20}$ (E) $\frac{17}{2}$

    (C) $\frac{17}{10}$

3. Write 4.6 as a percent.
    (A) 4.6%   (D) 46%
    (B) .46%   (E) 460%
    (C) .046%

4. Write $\frac{5}{12}$ as an equivalent percent.

    (A) 41%   (D) 4.1%

    (B) 41.6%   (E) $.41\frac{2}{3}\%$

    (C) $41\frac{2}{3}\%$

5. ·Write $\frac{1}{2}\%$ as a decimal.

(A) .5   (D) 50.0

(B) .005   (E) .05

(C) 5.0

How wise? Check your answers on page 111.

FINDING PERCENTS

An equation to commit to memory is: $\frac{\%}{100} = \frac{\text{part}}{\text{whole}}$. This proportion equation will help you solve almost any percent problem that comes your way. Another way to solve percent problems is to use the decimal equivalent. You'll see as you get better at percents that sometimes it's easier to just multiply by the decimal equivalents (due to all the large numbers you can get) than to set up a proportion.

Example 1: Find 32% of 84.

Method 1 Solution: Proportion   *Method 2 Solution:* Decimal

$$\frac{32}{100} = \frac{x}{84}$$

$$100x = 2688$$

$$x = 26.88$$

$$\begin{array}{r} 84 \\ \times.32 \\ \hline 168 \\ \underline{252} \\ 26.88 \end{array}$$

Both methods involved about as much work. Use the one you know better.

Sometimes you get a wacky fraction as a percent, and you can convert immediately if you've memorized the Conversion Chart on page 96.

Example 2: Find $12\frac{1}{2}\%$ of 112.

Method 1 Solution: Proportion

$$\frac{12\frac{1}{2}}{100} = \frac{x}{112}$$
$$100x = 1400$$
$$x = 14$$

Method 2 Solution: Decimal

$$\begin{array}{r} 112 \\ \times\ .125 \\ \hline 560 \\ 2240 \\ \underline{11200} \\ 14.000 \end{array}$$

So, which do you think is the easiest method? It really doesn't matter which one you choose as long as it's comfortable for you.

If you're stuck and can't figure out which method to use, or you just don't understand the methods at all, you can always use the failsafe math–English translation method. In this method, you simply rewrite the words into math symbols like you learned in Chapter 3: "*percent*" means "over 100"; "*is*" means "equals"; "*of*" means "times"; and "*what*" means an unknown quantity, or an *x*.

Example: Find $12\frac{1}{2}\%$ of 112.

Solution: Change $12\frac{1}{2}\%$ to $\frac{1}{8}$ (because you know your Conversion Chart!).

$$\frac{1}{8} \cdot \overset{14}{\cancel{112}} = 14$$

Try the math–English translation again:

Example: What is 30% of 40?

Solution: What (*x*) is (=) 30% ($\frac{30}{100}$) of (×) 40?

Aha! I knew that this was easier than my teachers made it sound. It's like translating Spanish to English. Each word stands for something else.

See how simple that is? Sometimes there's more math involved, but you will never go wrong if you do a direct translation.

Get Wise!

See if you can figure out how to find percents in the problems below. You can use any method you choose. If you're stuck, try a direct translation.

1. What is 40% of 40?
   - (A) .16
   - (B) 1.6
   - (C) 16
   - (D) 160
   - (E) 1600

2. What is 42% of 67?
   - (A) 2814
   - (B) 281.4
   - (C) 2.814
   - (D) .2814
   - (E) 28.14

3. Find $16\frac{2}{3}\%$ of 120.
   - (A) 20
   - (B) 2
   - (C) 200
   - (D) 16
   - (E) 32

4. What is $\frac{1}{5}\%$ of 40?
   - (A) 8
   - (B) .8
   - (C) .08
   - (D) .008
   - (E) .0008

5.   Find $r\%$ of s.

(A) $\dfrac{100s}{r}$ (D) $\dfrac{r}{100s}$

(B) $\dfrac{rs}{100}$ (E) $\dfrac{s}{100r}$

(C) $\dfrac{100r}{s}$

How wise? Check your answers on page 112.

FINDING THE BIG NUMBER

So far, we have had to find a percent of a given number. What if you have to find the number when you are given a percent of it? You can use the same methods from above. The main point to keep in mind is that no matter what method you like best—proportion, decimal, or direct translation—you are still writing the same facts from a math word problem into a math equation.

Example: 7 is 5% of what number?

Proportion Solution:

$$\frac{5}{100} = \frac{7}{x}$$
$$5x = 700$$
$$x = 140$$

Direct Translation Solution:

$$7 = 5/100 \cdot x$$
$$7 = 5x/100$$
$$700 = 5x$$
$$x = 140$$

Decimal Solution:

$$7 = .05x$$
$$700 = 5x$$
$$x = 140$$

WISE NOTE

Just think of the amount of time you'll save if you remember that $66\frac{2}{3}$% in a problem has a fraction equivalence of $\frac{2}{3}$, making it easier to use the proportion equation to solve it. Are you convinced yet that the Conversion Chart on page 96 should be memorized?

Get Wise!

Try some of these on your own. You can look at the chart for decimal equivalents to see if it saves you some time. You are hurrying to get through this, right?

1. 72 is 12% of what number?
   (A) 6
   (B) 60
   (C) 600
   (D) 86.4
   (E) 8.64

2. 80 is $12\frac{1}{2}$% of what number?
   (A) 10
   (B) 100
   (C) 64
   (D) 640
   (E) 6400

3. $37\frac{1}{2}$% of what number is 27?
   (A) 72
   (B) $10\frac{1}{8}$
   (C) 90
   (D) 101.25
   (E) 216

4. *m* is *p*% of what number?

   (A) $\dfrac{mp}{100}$ (D) $\dfrac{p}{100m}$

   (B) $\dfrac{100p}{m}$ (E) $\dfrac{100m}{p}$

   (C) $\dfrac{m}{100p}$

5. 50% of what number is *r*?

   (A) $\dfrac{1}{2}r$ (D) $2r$

   (B) $5r$ (E) $100r$

   (C) $10r$

How wise? Check your answers on page 112.

PERCENT INCREASE/DECREASE

The trickiest kind of percent problem involves increases and decreases. Honestly, they may seem tricky, we won't sugarcoat it. The trick is to memorize the simple formula. (Come on, we don't ask you to memorize much, do we? Maybe one thing per chapter . . .)

$$\text{Percent Increase/Decrease} = \frac{change}{original} \times 100$$

The *change* is the amount of dollars, people, monkeys, or whatever it is that *changes*.

Warning: You may have to do some subtraction here.

Oh, so the percent *change* is found by subtraction. Before cell phones, I used to check pay phones for change. And my father always says, "Change is good."

The *original* is the number where you start. In a percent *increase* problem, a number is getting bigger—so your *original* is the *smaller* number.

Example: There is an increase of enrollment in the key club because of the hot new president. Originally there were 15 members (it was lame). There are now 25 members. What is the percent increase?

Solution: Because of the superficial enrollment of 10 eager-to-date, hormone-filled teens who couldn't care less about community service and grades (but I digress), there is a boost in members from its original, and somewhat inadequate, 15. The percent is found by dividing $\dfrac{change}{original} = \dfrac{10}{15} = \dfrac{2}{3} = .\overline{6}$ and multiplying by 100. In this case, it's probably going to be correct if you write 67% (round up 66.666), or you can write it as a fraction: $66\dfrac{2}{3}$.

In a percent *decrease* problem, the *original* number is the larger number. That's because if it's decreasing, it was once bigger, right? Stick with us here, it's not rocket science.

Example: Music stores observed a decrease in sales for the latest boy-band CD after it was learned that the lead singer was really 42 and bald. Sales dropped from 180 CDs sold/week to 45. What was the percent decrease?

Solution: Ah, will the youth never learn that it is the old bald men who run this country? Anyway, the difference in sales is 135. (By the way, we made the numbers in the examples rather easy this time. Don't count on that in the practice to follow.) Therefore, your equation looks like this:

$$\frac{change}{original} = \frac{135}{180} = .75 \times 100 = 75\%.$$

But don't worry about the band—I'm sure they'll be fine in their new careers as actors.

Finally, follow us as we lead you on an example that will combine your powers of increase and decrease. You never know what those test makers will hit you with.

Example: Due to the studies done on the local nuclear power plant, Springfield Elementary experiences a student enrollment decrease of 20% of its 150 bright, young minds. By what percent must Principal Skinner now increase his enrollment for next year so that he won't lose money on the mystery meat sitting in the freezer all summer?

Solution: Tricky, tricky. First, you calculate how many youngsters have left in pursuit of fresher air and cleaner water fountains: 150 – 20% = 30. (If you don't remember, 10% is found by moving the decimal one place to the left (15). Then we double it, like you *should* do with a tip.) So, now there are 120 students.

If Skinner wants to lure 30 new unsuspecting children into the school of cancerous possibilities, he needs to find "what % of 120 is 30?" Your *original* number is now the one we already decreased. Try a direct translation of the part in quotes:

$$\frac{x}{100} \text{ (what percent)} \times \text{(of)} \ 120 = \text{(is)} \ 30?$$

The answer? 25%!!!

Get Wise!

Remember when we told you that the examples would work out nicely? Try your hand at these to see if you really understand the concept of percent increase/decrease.

1. Mrs. Morris receives a salary raise from $25,000 to $27,500. Find the percent of increase.

   (A) 9   (D) 15
   (B) 10   (F) 25
   (C) 90

2. The population of Stormville has increased from 80,000 to 100,000 in the last twenty years. Find the percent of increase.

   (A) 20   (D) 60
   (B) 25   (E) 10
   (C) 80

3. The value of Super Company Stock dropped from $25 a share to $21 a share. Find the percent of decrease.

   (A) 4   (D) 16
   (B) 8   (E) 20
   (C) 12

4. The Rubins bought their home for $30,000 and sold it for $60,000. What was the percent of increase?

   (A) 100   (D) 300
   (B) 50   (E) 150
   (C) 200

5. During the pre-holiday rush, Martin's Department Store increased its sales staff from 150 to 200 persons. By what percent must it now decrease its sales staff to return to the usual number of salespersons?

    (A) 25   (D) 40

    (B) $33\frac{1}{3}$ (E) 75

    (C) 20

How wise? Check your answers on page 113.

PROPORTIONS AND DIRECT TRANSLATIONS

The last kind of percent problem you'll see is when you're given a number and you need to find out how much percent it is of another number. It sounds more complicated than it is. Proportions and direct translations will get you the fastest answers here.

Example: 30 is what percent of 1500?

Proportion Solution:

$$\frac{x}{100} = \frac{30}{1500}$$
$$1500x = 3000$$
$$x = 2\%$$

Direct Translation Solution:
    (Remember—"what percent" means $x/100$.)

$$30 = \frac{x}{100} \times 1500$$
$$30 = \frac{1500x}{100}$$
$$30 = 15x$$
$$x = 2$$

Get Wise!

Try the problems below. Use any method you want to.

1. 4 is what percent of 80?
   (A) 20   (D) .5
   (B) 2   (E) 40
   (C) 5

2. $\frac{1}{2}$ of 6 is what percent of $\frac{1}{4}$ of 60?
   (A) 5   (D) 25
   (B) 20   (E) 15
   (C) 10

3. What percent of 96 is 12?
   (A) $16\frac{2}{3}$ (D) 8

   (B) $8\frac{1}{3}$ (E) $12\frac{1}{2}$

   (C) $37\frac{1}{2}$

4. What percent of 48 is 48?
   (A) 1   (D) 48
   (B) 10   (E) 0
   (C) 100

5. What percent of y is x?

    (A) $\dfrac{x}{y}$ (D) $\dfrac{100x}{y}$

    (B) $\dfrac{x}{100y}$ (E) $\dfrac{100y}{x}$

    (C) $\dfrac{xy}{100}$

How wise? Check your answers on page 114.

A Word to the Wise

Percents: The Vocabulary

★ Percent means "*out of 100.*"

★ In percent problems (as well as in all math problems) you can translate words into math symbols:

    "Of" means multiply.

    "Is" means an equals sign.

    "What" means a variable.

    "What percent" means $x/100$.

Percents: Switch Hitting

★ Percents can be written in many ways: $5\% = \dfrac{5}{100} = .05$

★ Percent problems should be solved using the method you are most comfortable with.

Percents: Know the Translations

★ Percents are easier and can be solved faster if you know the fraction and decimal equivalents. Memorize the Conversion Chart on page 96.

★ If a percent is *greater than 100*, the same rules apply. Remember that $100\% = 1$; $200\% = 2$; $300\% = 3$, and so on.

Percents: Increase/Decrease

★ The formula: $\dfrac{\text{Change}}{\text{Original}}$

★ The original number is the *smaller* total in an *increase* and the *larger* total in a *decrease* problem.

ANSWERS TO CHAPTER 5: PRACTICE EXERCISES

Conversions (Page 98)

1. **(C)** To change a percent to a decimal, move the decimal point two places to the *left*: $3\dfrac{1}{2}\% = 3.5\% = .035$

2. **(B)** $85\% = \dfrac{85}{100} = \dfrac{17}{20}$

3. **(E)** To change a decimal to a percent, move the decimal point two places to the *right:*

4. **(C)** To change a fraction to a percent, multiply by 100:

$$\dfrac{5}{\overset{}{\underset{3}{\cancel{12}}}} \cdot \overset{25}{\cancel{100}} = \dfrac{125}{3} = 41\dfrac{2}{3}\%$$

5. **(B)** $\dfrac{1}{2}\% = .5\% = .005$

Finding Percents (Page 101)

1. **(C)** $40\% = \dfrac{2}{5}$ (Straight off the conversion chart!)

$$\dfrac{2}{\cancel{5}_1} \cdot \cancel{40}^{8} = 16$$

2. **(E)**
$$
\begin{array}{r}
67 \\
\times\underline{.42} \\
1\,34 \\
\underline{26\,80} \\
28.14
\end{array}
$$

> **Decimals *are* easier to work with if you don't have a quick and easy fraction conversion!**

3. **(A)** $16\dfrac{2}{3}\% = \dfrac{1}{6}$

$$\dfrac{1}{\cancel{6}_1} \cdot \cancel{120}^{20} = 20$$

4. **(C)** $\dfrac{1}{5}\% = .2\% = .002$

Careful, fractions mean small, small percents!

$$
\begin{array}{r}
40 \\
\times\underline{.002} \\
.0800
\end{array}
$$

5. **(B)** $r\% = \dfrac{r}{100}$

$$\dfrac{r}{100} \cdot s = \dfrac{rs}{100}$$

Finding the Big Number: (Page 103)

1. **(C)**
$$72 = .12x$$
$$7200 = 12x$$
$$x = 600$$

2. **(D)** $80 = \dfrac{1}{8}x$

    $640 = x$

3. **(A)** $\dfrac{3}{8}x = 27$

    $3x = 216$

    $x = 72$

4. **(E)** $m = \dfrac{p}{100} \cdot x$

    $100m = px$

    $\dfrac{100m}{p} = x$

5. **(D)** $\dfrac{1}{2}x = r$

    $x = 2r$

Percent Increase/Decrease (Page 107)

1. **(B)** Amount of increase = $2500

    $$\text{Percent of increase} = \frac{\text{amount of increase}}{\text{original}}$$

    $\dfrac{2500}{25,000} = \dfrac{1}{10} = 10\%$

2. **(B)** Amount of increase = 20,000

    $\text{Percent of increase} = \dfrac{20,000}{80,000} = \dfrac{1}{4} = 25\%$

3. **(D)** Amount of decrease = $4

    $\text{Percent of decrease} = \dfrac{4}{25} = \dfrac{16}{100} = 16\%$

4. **(A)** Amount of increase = $30,000

    $\text{Percent of increase} = \dfrac{30,000}{30,000} = 1 = 100\%$

5. **(A)** Amount of decrease = 50

    $\text{Percent of decrease} = \dfrac{50}{200} = \dfrac{1}{4} = 25\%$

Proportions and Direct Translations (Page 109)

1. **(C)** $\dfrac{x}{100} = \dfrac{4}{80}$

    $80x = 400$

    $x = 5\%$

2. **(B)** $\dfrac{1}{2}$ of 6= 3

    $\dfrac{1}{4}$ of 60= 15

    $\dfrac{3}{15} = \dfrac{1}{5} = 20\%$

Use three steps. Be careful—organization is important!

3. **(E)** $\dfrac{12}{96} = \dfrac{1}{8} = 12\dfrac{1}{2}\%$

Conversion Chart, you are my hero.

4. **(C)** $\dfrac{48}{48} = 1 = 100\%$

Hey, that last problem was thrown in to see if you're paying attention. Are you? Doctors say that what you eat and how you play might affect your attention span. So I balance my diet and only play video games a few hours a day.

5. **(D)** $\dfrac{x}{y} \cdot 100 = \dfrac{100x}{y}$

chapter 6

The Laws of
the Average

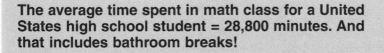

The average time spent in math class for a United States high school student = 28,800 minutes. And that includes bathroom breaks!

Being average might not be a goal for many teenagers; however, learning how to find averages should be. This chapter will teach you how to solve different types of average problems.

FINDING SIMPLE AVERAGES

When you were younger, you may have been taught an average problem such as this:

Example: On Monday, Mary went to the park and bought 5 balloons. On Tuesday and Wednesday she had only enough money to buy 2 balloons each day. On Thursday she got her allowance and splurged on 10 balloons. On Friday she bought 1 balloon. What was the average number of balloons Mary bought that week?

Solution: Sharing in Mary's love of new balloons, you dutifully added the totals of balloons for each day and divided by the amount of days: $5 + 2 + 2 + 10 + 1 = 20$, and $20 \div 5 = 4$.

Twenty Balloons?! What's up with that? I can think of a lot of other things I'd rather spend my allowance on, and balloons aren't even on the list!

Those were simple averages. Of course, you grew up and now not all problems are simple. Some require trickier knowledge. For example, if the numbers are in a series, the average will be the middle number.

Everything gets much more complicated as you get older. Remember when stress meant rushing to play outside after eating milk and cookies?

Example: Find the average of the first 20 positive even integers.

WISE NOTE

An *integer* is any positive or negative number, including 0, that has no fraction or numbers to the right of the decimal point.

Solution: Sure, you can write them all out, waste 8 minutes scribbling the even numbers from 2 to 40 while precious time ticks away, add them up, and divide by the amount of numbers you have, yada yada yada, and sure, you'll get the right answer—OR you can think for a minute. Since 1–40 equals 40 numbers and they do that alternating thing (where one is odd, the next is even) only half, or 20, of the 40 numbers are even. The two numbers in the middle of the even pack are 20 and 22. The average of those two numbers is 21. Interestingly, all the numbers paired in this fashion will get you 21. Look at the biggest and smallest (40, 2): their average is 21. Same with the next biggest and smallest (38, 4). See what we mean here? Amazing what you can figure out sometimes. And hey, if you didn't know it before, it's just another thing to add to that book of tricks you've got going!

One more thing: keep the *units* the same. For example, feet can only be averaged with feet, not with inches. Would you try to average the number of "Simpsons" reruns with "Felicity" reruns? No way! Same rules apply to averages. And fractions should be changed to decimals first—it's easier!

Example: Find the average of $87\frac{1}{2}\%$, $\frac{1}{4}$, and .6.

Solution: To solve for the average of these numbers, you must first convert to decimals. Rewrite as decimals, add, then divide by 3.

$$
\begin{array}{r}
.875 \\
.25 \\
+ .6 \\
\hline
1.725
\end{array}
$$

$$
\begin{array}{r}
.575 \\
3\overline{)1.725}
\end{array}
$$

Get Wise!

Ace the following average problems and you'll be better than average.

1. Find the average of $\sqrt{.49}$, $\frac{3}{4}$, and 80%.

   (A) .72   (D) .075

   (B) .75   (E) .073

   (C) .78

2. Find the average of the first 5 positive integers that end in 3.

   (A) 3   (D) 23

   (B) 13   (E) 28

   (C) 18

3. Hank's basketball team has 5 men who weigh 160, 185, 210, 200, and 195 pounds. Find the average weight of these players.

   (A) 190   (D) 198

   (B) 192   (E) 180

   (C) 195

4. Find the average of a, $2a$, $3a$, $4a$, and $5a$.

   (A) $3a^5$ (D) $2.8a^5$

   (B) $3a$ (E) 3

   (C) $2.8a$

5. Find the average of $\dfrac{1}{2}$, $\dfrac{1}{3}$, and $\dfrac{1}{4}$.

   (A) $\dfrac{1}{9}$ (D) $\dfrac{13}{12}$

   (B) $\dfrac{13}{36}$ (E) $\dfrac{1}{3}$

   (C) $\dfrac{1}{27}$

How wise? Check your answers on page 127.

I know the Conversion Chart on page 96 has decimal equivalents for these fractions. Fractions are fine, but decimals are just easier! Fractions have too many numbers and things to deal with. In math, less is best.

MISSING NUMBERS

Suppose you're given an average, but you're missing a number to be added with others and divided to find the average! It's still an average problem, you're just going to work it out backward this time.

Example: The average of 4 numbers is 26. If 3 of these numbers are 50, 12, and 28, find the missing fourth number.

Solution: So 4 numbers are added together and divided by 4 to get 26. You only know 3 of the numbers. Easy enough to find the fourth number; just call it x for now. Look at the logic: A total will be divided by 4 to get you 26, the average. So, $50 + 12 + 28 + x =$ total. What's the total? The total is 26×4, or 104.

Now it's a simple algebra problem:

$$(50 + 12 + 28) + x = 104$$
$$x = 104 - (50 + 12 + 28)$$
$$x = 14$$

Don't worry if you got a little lost up there! The average person will need to take some time and organize an intricate average problem to solve for a missing number. Just remember that the *total* is always what you get when you add the numbers. And the *total* is also equal to the average *times* the amount of numbers. Division merely reverses the process of multiplication! (Check out Chapter 1 for inverse functions if you forgot this—division and multiplication are inverse operations, just like addition and subtraction.)

Get Wise!

Scientists spent centuries trying to find the missing link. Try the average problems below to see if you can find the missing numbers.

1. Dave's average for his freshman year was 88, his sophomore year was 94, and his junior year was 91. If he wants to graduate with a 92 GPA, what does his average have to be senior year?

    (A) 92   (D) 95
    (B) 93   (E) 96
    (C) 94

If Dave up there actually thinks of all this stuff this far in advance, he has already achieved highest nerdom. College should be a breeze for him.

2. The average of X, Y, and another number is M. Find the missing number.

    (A) $3M - X + Y$ (D) $M - X - Y$
    (B) $3M - X - Y$ (E) $M - X + Y$

    (C) $\dfrac{M + X + Y}{3}$

Do you get brain freeze when you see variables? Shake the cold sweats by pretending they're real numbers and do your stuff!

3. The average of two numbers is $2x$. If one of the numbers is $x + 3$, find the other number.

   (A) $x - 3$ (D) -3

   (B) $2x - 3$ (E) $3x + 3$

   (C) $3x - 3$

4. The high temperatures in Arlin were $86°$, $82°$, $90°$, $92°$, $80°$, and $81°$. What was the high temperature on the 7th day if the average high for the week was $84°$?

   (A) $79°$ (D) $77°$

   (B) $85°$ (E) $76°$

   (C) $81°$

5. If the average of five consecutive integers is 17, find the largest of these integers.

   (A) 17   (D) 20

   (B) 18   (E) 21

   (C) 19

How wise? Check your answers on page 128.

AVERAGES THAT REPEAT

This final average section is to remind you to read problems carefully. Sometimes an average problem will tell you that a number occurs more than once. Just treat these numbers as separate entities and you'll have no trouble with finding averages.

Example: Bart drove for 6 hours at an average rate of 50 mph and he drove for 2 hours at an average rate of 60 mph. Find his average rate for the entire trip so he can brag to Otto.

Solution: Since Bart drove a total of 8 hours, we know we're looking to average 8 numbers. Logic also tells us that since he drove many more hours at a slower rate of 50 mph, his average should be closer to 50 rather than 60 (and probably not good enough to qualify for the under-13 NASCAR tournament)! The math looks like this:

$$\frac{6(50)+2(60)}{8} = \frac{300+120}{8} = \frac{420}{8} = 52\frac{1}{2} \text{ or } 52.5 \text{ mph}$$

Brag to Otto? What's there to brag about? Even my grandma drives faster than that!

Get Wise!

Try the following average problems:

1. In Mary Griffin's gym class, 6 girls weigh 120 pounds each, 8 girls weigh 125 pounds each, and 10 girls weigh 116 pounds each. What is the average weight of these clearly made-up girls?

    (A) 120 (D) 122
    (B) 118 (E) 119
    (C) 121

2. Dr. Nick drove for three hours at 60 miles per hour and for 4 hours at 55 miles per hour on his way to a transplant convention in Nevada. What was his average rate, in miles per hour, for the entire trip?

    (A) 57.5 (D) 58.2
    (B) 56.9 (E) 57.8
    (C) 57.1

3. In South Lark Elementary, five teachers earn $15,000 per year, three teachers earn $17,000 per year, and one teacher earns $18,000 per year. Find the average yearly salary of these struggling and underpaid civil servants.

    (A) $16,667 (D) $16,448
    (B) $16,000 (E) $16,025
    (C) $17,000

I'd better be nicer to my teachers. They can't even afford to see a shrink!

4. During the first four weeks of summer vacation, Kenny worked at a camp earning $50 per week. During the next six weeks of vacation,

he worked as a stock boy earning $100 per week. What was his average weekly pay for the summer?

(A) $80   (D) $83.33

(B) $75   (E) $82

(C) $87.50

5.   If *M* students each received a grade of *P* on a physics test ·and *N* students each received a grade of *Q*, what was the average grade for this group of students?

(A) $\dfrac{P+Q}{M+N}$ (D) $\dfrac{MP+NQ}{P+Q}$

(B) $\dfrac{PQ}{M+N}$ (E) $\dfrac{M+N}{P+Q}$

(C) $\dfrac{MP+NQ}{M+N}$

How wise? Check your answers on page 128.

A Word to the Wise

Averages: The Facts

★ *Averages* are found by adding up the numbers and dividing by the amount of numbers.

★ The average of an *evenly spaced series of numbers* is the number in the middle.

★ To find a *number missing* from an average problem:

1.   Total the numbers you know.

2.   Multiply the amount of numbers by the average.

3.   Subtract step 1 from step 2.

★ Remember, some average word problems will tell you a certain number occurs more than once, so *read carefully.*

ANSWERS TO CHAPTER 6: PRACTICE EXERCISES

Finding Simple Averages (Page 120)

1. **(B)** $\sqrt{.49} = .7$

$$\frac{3}{4} = .75$$

$$80\% = +\underline{.80}$$

$$2.25$$

$$3\overline{)2.25} \quad \begin{array}{c} .75 \end{array}$$

2. **(D)** The integers are 3, 13, 23, 33, 43. Since these are evenly spaced, the average is the middle integer, 23.

3. **(A)** $160 + 185 + 210 + 200 + 195 = 950$

$$\frac{950}{5} = 190$$

4. **(B)** These numbers are evenly spaced (You should be getting the hang of this by now!), so the average is the middle number, $3a$.

5. **(B)** $\dfrac{1}{2} + \dfrac{1}{3} + \dfrac{1}{4} = \dfrac{6}{12} + \dfrac{4}{12} + \dfrac{3}{12} = \dfrac{13}{12}$

To divide this sum by 3, multiply by $\dfrac{1}{3}$:

$$\frac{13}{12} \cdot \frac{1}{3} = \frac{13}{36}$$

Missing Numbers (Page 122)

1. **(D)** His goal is 92. The total is the average times the number of numbers, or $92 \times 4 = 368$. When you add all four years' GPAs, you should get 368. Since this was #1 you're allowed to make a mistake, but come on, this one was pretty easy, right? $88 + 94 + 91 + \underline{95} = 368$

2. **(B)** $\dfrac{X + Y + x}{3} = M$

    $$X + Y + x = 3M$$
    $$x = 3M - X - Y$$

3. **(C)** Here we're going to use n as the variable we don't know since x is already used in the problem:

    $$\frac{(x+3)+n}{2} = 2x$$
    $$x + 3 + n = 4x$$
    $$n = 3x - 3$$

4. **(D)** The average high in Arlin was 84. So your Total is $84 \times 7 = 588$. If you add choice (D), 77, to the other 6 days' highs, you will get 588.

5. **(C)** 17 must be the middle integer, since the five integers are consecutive and the average is, like we said before, the middle number. The numbers are 15, 16, 17, 18, and 19.

Averages That Repeat (Page 125)

1. **(A)** Add the 24 girls' weights and divide by 24:

    $$6(120) = 720$$
    $$8(125) = 1000$$
    $$10(116) = \underline{1160}$$
    $$2880$$

    $$24\overline{)2880}$$
    $$120$$

2.　**(C)**　Add the 7 hours of rates and divide by 7:

$$3(60) = 180$$
$$4(55) = \underline{220}$$
$$\qquad\quad 400$$

$$7\overline{)\quad 400}^{\;57.142} \approx 57.1$$

Round off the decimal to find that the answer is (C), 57.1.

3.　**(B)**　$5(15,000) = 75,000$

$\qquad\quad 3(17,000) = 51,000$

$\qquad\quad 1(18,000) = \underline{18,000}$

$\qquad\qquad\qquad\quad\; 144,000$

$$9\overline{)144,000}^{\;16,000}$$

4.　**(A)**　$4(50) \;\; = 200$

$\qquad\quad 6(100) \;\; = \underline{600}$

$\qquad\qquad\qquad\; 800$

$$10\overline{)800}^{\;80}$$

5.　**(C)**　$M(P) = MP$

$\qquad\quad N(Q) = \underline{NQ}$

$\qquad\qquad\qquad MP + NQ$

Divide by the number of students, $M + N$, so the correct answer is

$$\frac{MP + NQ}{M + N}.$$

chapter 7

Roots and Exponents

Roots—also called *radicals*—are easy to work with once you know the rules. Just like those pesky gardening roots of another kind, there are simple rules for handling their elimination. Without guidelines, you'd go crazy with these guys, treat them incorrectly, and get stuck in a maze of spuds and duds. The basic rule is "Treat roots as a unit." This means you can't just add the roots together.

Somewhere in your math education you were probably forced to memorize the simple square roots. We hope you remember some of them. Knowing that $6^2 = 36$ and $\sqrt{81} = 9$ will lessen the reliance on calculators. The squares of numbers 1 through 12 are most useful.

Squares are useful to know, but not nearly as useful as my new RetroRed Lip Gloss, fast food, and my purple Discman with "invisible" headphones.

ADDITION AND SUBTRACTION

Technically, you can't add or subtract what's underneath the radical sign, but you *can* work with their *coefficients*. Those are the numbers in front of the funky check sign, like the numbers next to variables. Coefficient is Latin and means a relationship exists between it and what it's next to—supposedly, an *efficient* relationship. But its efficiency, dear learner, will depend on how you use it.

Example: $4\sqrt{2} + 5\sqrt{2} = 9\sqrt{2}$ because the two numbers you are adding both have a square root of 2. However, $4\sqrt{2} + 5\sqrt{3}$ has two different roots, so they cannot be combined.

Simplifying Roots

Of course, you can easily work with roots if you figure out what to pull out from under the radical sign. The number underneath represents a product of all its factors. You need to look at $\sqrt{150}$ as if a 5, a 6, and another 5 are all under there, multiplying with each other. To simplify a root, you take out factors that appear twice. Numbers that are in there alone cannot be uprooted. Think of them as unripened radishes that must grow in the soil for another season.

Example: $\sqrt{30} = \sqrt{5} \cdot \sqrt{6}$
$\sqrt{150} = \sqrt{6} \cdot \sqrt{25} = 5\sqrt{6}$

Now, if you're asked to find $\sqrt{125} + \sqrt{20} - \sqrt{500}$, you first need to simplify each one:

$$\sqrt{25} \cdot \sqrt{5} + \sqrt{4} \cdot \sqrt{5} - \sqrt{100} \cdot \sqrt{5}$$

Then pull out the perfect squares: $5\sqrt{5} + 2\sqrt{5} - 10\sqrt{5}$

"Perfect square"? Isn't that an oxymoron? If someone's a square, they're certainly *not* perfect.

Nice how it worked out to all have $\sqrt{5}$, huh? (Sometimes we try to make your life easier.)

Life would be a heck of a lot easier if I knew the difference between a gardening handbook and a book on "roots." I think I stumbled into a twilight zone.

Then work with your coefficients: $5 + 2 - 10 = -3$. The answer is $-3\sqrt{5}$.

Get Wise!

Try the addition and subtraction of the roots below. Then we'll move on to hard stuff.

1. Combine $4\sqrt{27} - 2\sqrt{48} + \sqrt{147}$.

    (A) $27\sqrt{3}$ (D) $10\sqrt{3}$

    (B) $-3\sqrt{3}$ (E) $11\sqrt{3}$

    (C) $9\sqrt{3}$

2. Combine $\sqrt{80} + \sqrt{45} - \sqrt{20}$.

    (A) $9\sqrt{5}$ (D) $3\sqrt{5}$

    (B) $5\sqrt{5}$ (E) $-2\sqrt{5}$

    (C) $-\sqrt{5}$

3. Combine $6\sqrt{5} + 3\sqrt{2} - 4\sqrt{5} + \sqrt{2}$.

    (A) 8 (D) $5\sqrt{7}$

    (B) $2\sqrt{5} + 3\sqrt{2}$ (E) 5

    (C) $2\sqrt{5} + 4\sqrt{2}$

4. Combine $\frac{1}{2} \cdot \sqrt{180} + \frac{1}{3} \cdot \sqrt{45} - \frac{2}{5} \cdot \sqrt{20}$.

(A) $3\sqrt{10} + \sqrt{15} + 2\sqrt{2}$ (D) $\frac{24}{5}\sqrt{5}$

(B) $\frac{16}{5}\sqrt{5}$ (E)   none of these

(C) $\sqrt{97}$

What kind of answer choice is "none of these"? Come on, at least *real* answer choices give me something to aim for!

5. Combine $5\sqrt{mn} - 3\sqrt{mn} - 2\sqrt{mn}$.
   (A) 0   (D) mn

   (B) 1   (E) $-\sqrt{mn}$

   (C) $\sqrt{mn}$

How wise? Check your answers on page 143.

EXPONENTS

Before you can start on advanced root functions, such as multiplication and division, you need to master *exponents*. These little numbers written up and to the right of their coefficients stand for power! Remember, the order of operations tells us that these exponents must be solved first, with parentheses, so act wisely.

WISE NOTE

Other symbols of POWER: Superman's S, a gavel, Shaq's slam dunk, magic wands, this book.

When working with exponents, weird rules apply. To multiply them, you add them. To divide them, you subtract them.

Example: $\dfrac{5^{12} \cdot 5^5}{5^{14}} = \dfrac{5^{17}}{5^{14}} = 5^3 = 125$

Simple! Try this one:

Example: Solve $3^2 \cdot 2^3$

Solution: $3^2 \cdot 2^3 = 9 \cdot 8 = 72$

One major mistake often made with exponents is that students want to multiply the coefficients *before* figuring out the exponents. But you won't do that because:

1. You know your order of operations.

2. We just told you not to.

If you had multiplied coefficients first and then added exponents, you would get an insanely huge number: $6^5 = 7776$, which is no where near 72!

To raise an exponent to a power, you multiply them. You can either first distribute (use the exponent's power on the individual numbers in parentheses) or you can solve the parentheses first. Either way, it's all good.

Get Wise! Mastering Math Skills

Example: $\dfrac{\left(4^2 \cdot 4^4\right)^3}{\left(4^{10}\right)^2} = \dfrac{\left(4^6\right)^3}{\left(4\right)^{20}} = \dfrac{4^{18}}{4^{20}} = \dfrac{1}{4^2} = \dfrac{1}{16}$

or

$$\dfrac{\left(4^2 \cdot 4^4\right)^3}{\left(4^{10}\right)^2} = \dfrac{\left(4^6 \cdot 4^{12}\right)}{4^{20}} = \dfrac{4^{18}}{4^{20} \cdot} = \dfrac{1}{4^2} = \dfrac{1}{16}$$

MULTIPLICATION AND DIVISION

We were kidding about it becoming harder in this chapter. You already know how to work your roots, and in multiplication and division you have free reign to go crazy. Remember, there are only factors under there.

Example: $\sqrt{2} \cdot \sqrt{3} = \sqrt{6}$

Example: $4\sqrt{2} \cdot 5\sqrt{3} = 20 \cdot \sqrt{6}$ Multiply coefficients and roots separately!

To raise a root and its coefficient to a power, you raise the coefficient and root separately also.

This raises another question on roots: If my mom and dad were both bad math students, is it in my *roots* that I will also? I'll have to check on that.

Example: $(3\sqrt{2})^2 = 3\sqrt{2} \cdot 3\sqrt{2} = 9 \cdot 2 = 18$

Now look at division!

Now we're learning how to divide radicals. Webster's says *division* means "the act of separating and keeping apart," and *radical* means "an advocate of political or social revolution"— hmm, keeping apart advocates of political revolution? So, math even includes political propaganda? Maybe I'll get extra credit if I show this to my history teacher!

Example: $\dfrac{\sqrt{8}}{\sqrt{2}} = \sqrt{4} = 2$

Example: Divide coefficients and roots separately: $\dfrac{10\sqrt{20}}{2\sqrt{4}} = 5\sqrt{5}$

Example: Distribute and simplify:

$$\sqrt{2}(\sqrt{8} + \sqrt{18}) = \sqrt{16} + \sqrt{36} = 4 + 6 = 10$$

Get Wise!

Work out the problems below.

1. Multiply and simplify: $2\sqrt{18} \cdot 6\sqrt{2}$

   (A) 72

   (B) 48

   (C) $12\sqrt{6}$

   (D) $8\sqrt{6}$

   (E) 36

2. Find $\left(3\sqrt{3}\right)^3$.

    (A) $27\sqrt{3}$ (D) $9\sqrt{3}$

    (B) $81\sqrt{3}$ (E) 243

    (C) 81

3. Multiply and simplify: $\dfrac{1}{2}\sqrt{2}(\sqrt{6} + \dfrac{1}{2}\sqrt{2})$

    (A) $\sqrt{3} + \dfrac{1}{2}$ (D) $\sqrt{6} + \dfrac{1}{.2}$

    (B) $\dfrac{1}{2} \cdot \sqrt{3}$ (E) $\sqrt{6} + 2$

    (C) $\sqrt{6} + 1$

4. Divide and simplify: $\dfrac{\sqrt{32b^3}}{\sqrt{8b}}$

    (A) $2\sqrt{b}$ (D) $\sqrt{2b^2}$

    (B) $\sqrt{2b}$ (E) $b\sqrt{2b}$

    (C) $2b$

5. Divide and simplify: $\dfrac{15\sqrt{96}}{5\sqrt{2}}$

    (A) $7\sqrt{3}$ (D) $12\sqrt{3}$

    (B) $7\sqrt{12}$ (E) $40\sqrt{3}$

    (C) $11\sqrt{3}$

How wise? Check your answers on page 144.

WORKING UNDER THE ROOTS

Technically, under the roots is dirt and more dirt, all the way to China. But with math roots, you don't have to dig too deep. You can always add or subtract numbers underneath the radical sign and leave it at that.

Example: $\sqrt{16+9} = \sqrt{25} = 5$

Interestingly, you *cannot* find the square root of each term separately: If $\sqrt{16+9} = \sqrt{16} + \sqrt{9}$, you would get 4 + 3, or 7. Since we just did the problem the *right* way and got 5, I think you know what needs to be done.

This is how it looks with fractions and variables.

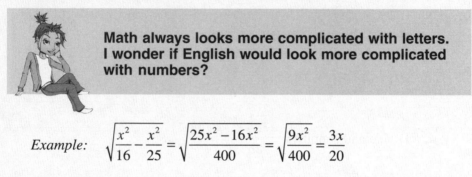

Math always looks more complicated with letters. I wonder if English would look more complicated with numbers?

Example: $\sqrt{\dfrac{x^2}{16} - \dfrac{x^2}{25}} = \sqrt{\dfrac{25x^2 - 16x^2}{400}} = \sqrt{\dfrac{9x^2}{400}} = \dfrac{3x}{20}$

If you remember from Chapter 2, fractions are subtracted easily by putting cross-products over a denominator product. Refresh as you need to, please; we don't want to sound redundant. We tried to explain that math is cumulative.

Get Wise!

Work out the root problems.

1. Simplify $\sqrt{\dfrac{x^2}{9} + \dfrac{x^2}{16}}$.

   (A) $\dfrac{25x^2}{144}$ (D) $\dfrac{x}{7}$

   (B) $\dfrac{5x}{12}$ (E) $\dfrac{7x}{12}$

   (C) $\dfrac{5x^2}{12}$

2. Simplify $\sqrt{36y^2 + 64x^2}$.

   (A) $6y + 8x$ (D) $10x^2y^2$

   (B) $10xy$ (E) cannot be done

   (C) $6y^2 + 8x^2$

3. Simplify $\sqrt{\dfrac{x^2}{64} - \dfrac{x^2}{100}}$.

   (A) $\dfrac{x}{40}$ (D) $\dfrac{3x}{40}$

   (B) $-\dfrac{x}{2}$ (E) $\dfrac{3x}{80}$

   (C) $\dfrac{x}{2}$

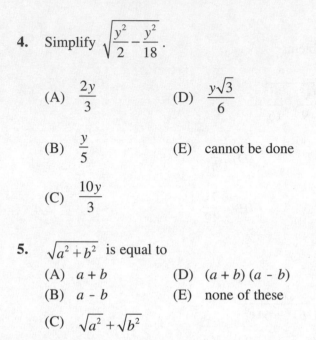

4. Simplify $\sqrt{\dfrac{y^2}{2} - \dfrac{y^2}{18}}$.

   (A) $\dfrac{2y}{3}$ (D) $\dfrac{y\sqrt{3}}{6}$

   (B) $\dfrac{y}{5}$ (E) cannot be done

   (C) $\dfrac{10y}{3}$

5. $\sqrt{a^2 + b^2}$ is equal to

   (A) $a + b$ (D) $(a + b)\,(a - b)$
   (B) $a - b$ (E) none of these
   (C) $\sqrt{a^2} + \sqrt{b^2}$

How wise? Check your answers on page 145.

FINDING SQUARE ROOTS

In finding the square root of a number, the first step is to pair off the digits in the square root sign in each direction from the decimal point. So, if there is an odd number of digits *before* the decimal point, insert a zero at the *beginning* of the number in order to pair digits. If an odd number of digits exists *after* the decimal point, add a zero at the *end*. It should be clearly understood that these zeros are place holders only and in no way change the value of the number. Every *pair* of numbers in the radical sign yields one digit of the square root.

It's all true, of course. And what it's trying to say is that if you're asked to find the square root of an insanely huge number, good luck. Just kidding again. Say your task is to find the square root of 328,329. A trick is to look at the multiple-choice answers (if your test has them!) for a three-digit number. See, every pair of numbers in a big number corresponds to one number in its root:

   (32)(83)(29)—3 pairs = 3 digits in square root

My roots need to be paired off and dyed soon. I'm thinking maybe fuschia. Since Tanya went with purple, I can't. I'd look like I worship her or something. And she knew I wanted purple, too.

What if you're asked to find the square root of 2,698,501, you ask? An odd amount of digits doesn't pair off! No worries, the first guy (2) stands alone. He also gets his own root correspondent:

(2)(69)(85)(01)—4 parentheses pairs = 4 digits in square root

TRICK OF THE TRADE

Of course, the fun begins when you find more than one answer choice with the amount of digits you need. This calls for more tricks. Before you call Harry Houdini, read on. We just might have what you're looking for.

Our first example, 328,329, ended in a 9. That means the square root must end in either a 3, since $3^2 = 9$, or a 7, since $7^2 = 49$. Getting the idea?

Example: The square root of 4624 is exactly

    (A) 64   (D) 67

    (B) 65   (E) 68

    (C) 66

Solution: A 4-digit number gives us a 2-digit root, but that doesn't help narrow it down. Use the last digit trick to see that only (E) ends in a number that, when squared, will give you a 4 in the units place: $8^2 = 64$.

Get Wise!

Use the last digit trick to solve the following problems.

1. The square root of 17,689 is exactly

    (A) 131   (D) 134

    (B) 132   (E) 136

    (C) 133

2. The number of digits in the square root of 64,048,009 is

    (A) 4   (D) 7

    (B) 5   (E) 8

    (C) 6

3. The square root of 222.01 is exactly

    (A) 14.3   (D) 14.8

    (B) 14.4   (E) 14.9

    (C) 14.6

4. The square root of 25.6036 is exactly

    (A) 5.6   (D) 5.0006

    (B) 5.06   (E) 5.00006

    (C) 5.006

5. Which of the following square roots can be found exactly?

    (A) $\sqrt{.4}$ (D) $\sqrt{.02}$

    (B) $\sqrt{.9}$ (E) $\sqrt{.025}$

    (C) $\sqrt{.09}$

How wise? Check your answers on page 145.

A Word to the Wise

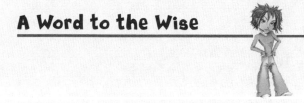

★ *Roots* are the same as *radicals*.

★ You can only *add* or *subtract* the coefficients of roots—and only if the numbers underneath the radical signs are the same: $5\sqrt{2} + 3\sqrt{2} = 8\sqrt{2}$ but $\sqrt{2} + \sqrt{7} \neq \sqrt{9}$.

★ To *simplify* a root, remember the number underneath is a product of its factors. Any factor you find in there twice can be pulled out and used as a coefficient.

   Example: $\sqrt{63} = \sqrt{3} \cdot \sqrt{3} \cdot \sqrt{7} = 3\sqrt{7}$

★ Feel free to *multiply* or *divide* roots as you would any common integer. Multiply and divide coefficients *separately* from numbers under the radical signs.

★ A trick to find the *root of a BIG number* is to *pair the digits*. Each pair corresponds to ONE digit of its square. To narrow it down further, look at the *squares of the units' digits* in the answer choices. In the correct answer, the units' digit of the square will match the units' digit in your problem.

ANSWERS TO CHAPTER 7: PRACTICE EXERCISES

Addition and Subtraction (Page 132)

1. **(E)** Simplify each quantity: $4\sqrt{27} = 4\sqrt{9} \cdot \sqrt{3} = 12\sqrt{3}$
$$2\sqrt{48} = 2\sqrt{16} \cdot \sqrt{3} = 8\sqrt{3}$$
$$\sqrt{147} = \sqrt{49} \cdot \sqrt{3} = 7\sqrt{3}$$

   Then rewrite as:
$$12\sqrt{3} - 8\sqrt{3} + 7\sqrt{3} = 11\sqrt{3}$$

2.   **(B)** $\sqrt{80} = \sqrt{16} \cdot \sqrt{5} = 4\sqrt{5}$

$\sqrt{45} = \sqrt{9} \cdot \sqrt{5} = 3\sqrt{5}$

$\sqrt{20} = \sqrt{4} \cdot \sqrt{5} = 2\sqrt{5}$

$4\sqrt{5} + 3\sqrt{5} - 2\sqrt{5} = 5\sqrt{5}$

See how they all simplify to have the same root?

3.   **(C)** Did we trick you? Only terms with the same root can be combined.

$$6\sqrt{5} - 4\sqrt{5} = 2\sqrt{5}$$
$$3\sqrt{2} + \sqrt{2} = 4\sqrt{2}$$

Therefore, we have $2\sqrt{5} + 4\sqrt{2}$.

4.   **(B)** $\frac{1}{2} \cdot \sqrt{180} = \frac{1}{2} \cdot \sqrt{36} \cdot \sqrt{5} = 3\sqrt{5}$

$$\frac{1}{3} \cdot \sqrt{45} = \frac{1}{3} \cdot \sqrt{9} \cdot \sqrt{5} = \sqrt{5}$$

$$\frac{2}{5} \cdot \sqrt{20} = \frac{2}{5} \cdot \sqrt{4} \cdot \sqrt{5} = \frac{4}{5}\sqrt{5}$$

$$3\sqrt{5} + \sqrt{5} - \frac{4}{5} \cdot \sqrt{5} = 4\sqrt{5} - \frac{4}{5}\sqrt{5}$$

$$= 3\frac{1}{5}\sqrt{5} = \frac{16}{5}\sqrt{5}$$

5.   **(A)** $5\sqrt{mn} - 5\sqrt{mn} = 0$ We wanted to save space!

Multiplication and Division (Page 136)

1.   **(A)** $2\sqrt{18} \cdot 6\sqrt{2} = 12\sqrt{36} = 12 \cdot 6 = 72$ See? Multiplication *is* easier!

2.   **(B)**   Expand it out! $3\sqrt{3} \cdot 3\sqrt{3} \cdot 3\sqrt{3} = 27(3\sqrt{3}) = 81 \cdot \sqrt{3}$

3. **(A)** Use the distributive law:

$$\frac{1}{2}\sqrt{12} + \frac{1}{4} \cdot 2 = \frac{1}{2}\sqrt{4} \cdot \sqrt{3} + \frac{1}{2} = \sqrt{3} + \frac{1}{2}$$

4. **(C)** Divide the numbers under radical sign: $\sqrt{4b^2} = 2b$

5. **(D)** Divide separately: $3\sqrt{48} = 3\sqrt{16} \cdot \sqrt{3} = 12\sqrt{3}$

Working under the Roots (Page 139)

1. **(B)** Cross-multiply up: $\sqrt{\dfrac{16x^2 + 9x^2}{144}} = \sqrt{\dfrac{25x^2}{144}} = \dfrac{5x}{12}$

2. **(E)** The terms cannot be combined and it is not possible to take the square root of separated terms.

3. **(D)** Cross-multiply up: $\sqrt{\dfrac{100x^2 - 64x^2}{6400}} = \sqrt{\dfrac{36x^2}{6400}} = \dfrac{6x}{80} = \dfrac{3x}{40}$

4. **(A)** Again: $\sqrt{\dfrac{18y^2 - 2y^2}{36}} = \sqrt{\dfrac{16y^2}{36}} = \dfrac{4y}{6} = \dfrac{2y}{3}$

5. **(E)** If you got nervous here and chose (D), calm down, you'll catch on soon. If you picked (A) or (B), what planet have you been on anyway? Choosing (C) is inexcusable: $\sqrt{16} + \sqrt{9} \neq \sqrt{25}$, remember?

Trick of the Trade (Page 142)

1. **(C)** We showed you one just like this. Since the last digit is 9, the square root must end in 3 or 7.

2. **(A)** Pair the digits. Count the pairs.

3. **(E)** Since the number ends in 1, its square root must end in 1 or 9.

4. **(B)** Pair the digits. Also, since the number has four digits to the right of the decimal, its square root has two digits to the right of the decimal.

5. **(C)** In order to take the square root of a decimal, it must have an even number of decimal places so that its square root will have half as many—the pair trick in reverse! And remember, the root must be a perfect square, and (D) doesn't immediately jump to mind as squares. So, only (C) works: $(\sqrt{.09} = .3)$.

chapter 8
Fractions with Variables

SIMPLIFYING ALGEBRAIC FRACTIONS

Simplify? Sounds strange, huh? What that actually means is making a problem, or fraction, *simpler*. And who doesn't want to simplify his or her life, right? Think about the millions of dollars a year spent on pop-psychology books that claim to "simplify" life! This is big business. And in this chapter, you're going to learn how to make math simple.

First, look at a fraction like $\frac{9}{12}$. If you can see that a factor of 3 can be taken out of the top and bottom (remember, you can't do one without the other), then you're on your way to fraction simplification already. Confused? Look at the math: $\frac{9}{12} = \frac{3 \cdot 3}{3 \cdot 4}$. And since the goal here is *simplification*, it is a simpler fraction if you get rid of those threes on top and on bottom. You can do that

---

147

because the multiplication of a 3 is canceled in the numerator and in the

denominator, like this: $\dfrac{9}{12} = \dfrac{\cancel{3} \cdot 3}{\cancel{3} \cdot 4} = \dfrac{3}{4}$

WISE NOTE

You can only simplify a fraction by canceling out its factors on top and on bottom. Trying to use addition, subtraction, or neglecting the top or bottom is sketchy simplification and simply wrong.

What if there are letters, you ask? Easy—keep in mind what you've just learned about simplification.

Example: $\dfrac{9t}{12t} = \dfrac{9\cancel{t}}{12\cancel{t}} = \dfrac{9}{12} = \dfrac{3}{4}$ Easy! The t variables canceled out!

Example: $\dfrac{9+t}{12+t}$ This fraction cannot be simplified.

No factor divides into the *entire* numerator and *entire* denominator. It would be incorrect to try to take out a 3 or a t because you can't pull a factor of 3 or t out of the quantity on the top or bottom. $(9 + t)$ is just $(9 + t)$. It would be wrong to think $3(3 + t)$ is the same thing, since that would be equal to $9 + 3t$ when the 3 is distributed. See?

So what other fractions *can be* simplified? Well, ones that look like the next example, of course.

Example: Simplify $\dfrac{4b^2 + 8b}{3b^3 + 6b^2}$.

Solution: Factor the numerator and denominator by removing the largest common factor in both. On top it's $4b$ and on bottom it's $3b^2$:

$$\frac{4b(b+2)}{3b^2(b+2)} = \frac{4\cancel{b}\,\cancel{(b+2)}}{3b\cdot\cancel{b}\,\cancel{(b+2)}}$$. Now you can see that the common

factors of both numerator and denominator are b and $(b+2)$.

Cancel them out and you are left with $\dfrac{4}{3b}$.

So this boy is walking with his mom and announces, "When I grow up I want to be a vitamin." Puzzled, she tells him that's impossible. The little boy insists this is not true and points to a sign in the window of a nearby store: Vitamin B1. "See?" he replies.

Example: Simplify $\dfrac{x^2+6x+8}{x^2+x-12}$.

There are no common factors here, but did you notice that there are THREE numbers on top and bottom? This means it can be factored as a *trinomial*. There is a special formula for this called FOIL, which you'll use again in chapter 9.

WISE NOTE

FOIL stands for "First, Outer, Inner, Last." This is the order in which you multiply two quantities together when they have 2 terms in them. Thus:

$(a + b)(c + d) = ac$ (First) + ad (Outer) + bc (Inner) + bd (Last)

With a mixture of numbers and one variable, you'll see that it's easy and that the inner and outer terms will combine when you multiply. Then you'll end up with a trinomial:

$(x + 4)(x + 2) = x^2 + 2x + 4x + 8 = x^2 + 6x + 8$

Solution: This problem factors into $\dfrac{(x+4)(x+2)}{(x+4)(x-3)}$ and you can cancel

out the $(x + 4)$ quantity. You're left with $\dfrac{(x+2)}{(x-3)}$ as a final an-

swer. Remember, you can't touch those x variables because they're *terms* and not *factors*.

Example: Simplify $\dfrac{10-2x}{x^2-4x-5}$.

Solution: The numerator contains a common factor: 2. But the denominator must be factored as a trinomial: $(x - 5)(x + 1)$. This is

what it looks like now: $\dfrac{2(5-x)}{(x-5)(x+1)}$.

Wait, there's more. Does a quantity on top *kind of* look like one on the bottom? You betcha. See, if numbers are reversed around subtraction like the $(5 - x)$ and $(x - 5)$, you can cancel out a term by multiplying one by (-1), which switches it around. Now

the problem looks like: $\dfrac{-2(x-5)}{(x-5)(x+1)}$, which simplifies to

$\dfrac{-2}{(x+1)}$.

Get Wise!

Find the simplest form for the fractions below.

1. Simplify $\dfrac{3x^3 - 3x^2y}{9x^2 - 9xy}$.

   (A) $\dfrac{x}{6}$ (D) 1

   (B) $\dfrac{x}{3}$ (E) $\dfrac{x-y}{3}$

   (C) $\dfrac{2x}{3}$

2. Simplify $\dfrac{2x-8}{12-3x}$.

   (A) $-\dfrac{2}{3}$ (D) $\dfrac{4}{3}$

   (B) $\dfrac{2}{3}$ (E) $-\dfrac{3}{2}$

   (C) $-\dfrac{4}{3}$

3. Find the value of $\dfrac{3x-y}{y-3x}$ when $x = \dfrac{2}{7}$ and $y = \dfrac{3}{10}$, $y \neq 3x$.

   (A) $\dfrac{24}{70}$ (D) 1

   (B) $\dfrac{11}{70}$ (E) -1

   (C) 0

4. Simplify $\dfrac{b^2 + b - 12}{b^2 + 2b - 15}$.

   (A) $\dfrac{4}{5}$

   (D) $\dfrac{b-4}{b-5}$

   (B) $-\dfrac{4}{3}$

   (E) $-\dfrac{b+4}{b+5}$

   (C) $\dfrac{b+4}{b+5}$

5. Simplify $\dfrac{2x + 4y}{6x + 12y}$.

   (A) $\dfrac{2}{3}$

   (D) $\dfrac{1}{3}$

   (B) $-\dfrac{2}{3}$

   (E) 3

   (C) $-\dfrac{1}{3}$

How wise? Check your answers on page 165.

A REVIEW OF BASIC OPERATIONS

We know you worked hard in Chapter 2 to master working with fractions, so we'll make this brief. Just treat the variables as if they were numbers.

Addition and Subtraction

To add or subtract, you need the same denominator. Remember that $\frac{a}{b} + \frac{c}{d} = \frac{ad+bc}{bd}$ and that $\frac{a}{b} - \frac{c}{d} = \frac{ad-bc}{bd}$. Look familiar? And please, simplify them or you might as well be mixing the batter and not pouring the pancakes.

Example: Add $\frac{3}{a} + \frac{2}{b}$.

Solution: Add the two cross products and put the sum over the denominator product: $\frac{3b+2a}{ab}$

Example: Add $\frac{2a}{3} + \frac{4a}{5}$.

Solution: Cross-multiply again and put it over the denominator product:

$$\frac{10a+12a}{15} = \frac{22a}{15}.$$

Not challenging enough? OK, we'll let you use more brainpower.

Example: Add $\frac{5a}{a+b} + \frac{5b}{a+b}$.

Solution: Aha—did you catch that they have the same denominator? Not hard. Add the numerators and put it over $(a + b)$. Don't run away yet, though; you'll need to simplify:

$$\frac{5a+5b}{a+b} = \frac{5(a+b)}{a+b} = 5$$

Look how that works out all clean as a whistle.

There are some phrases adults use that make no sense. Are whistles really clean? Do lambs shake their tails quickly? Are buttons cute? Were things really like that in the Stone Age?

Example: Subtract $\dfrac{4r-s}{6} - \dfrac{2r-7s}{6}$.

Solution: Here we're trying to show you that the minus sign will change the signs of the terms in the second numerator. It looks easy, because both fractions have the same denominator, but remember to take care with that subtraction sign:

$$\frac{4r-s-(2r-7s)}{6} = \frac{4r-s-2r+7s}{6} = \frac{2r+6s}{6} = \frac{2(r+3s)}{6} = \frac{r+3s}{3}$$

Get Wise!

Add and subtract the following fractions.

1. Subtract $\dfrac{6x+5y}{2x} - \dfrac{4x+y}{2x}$.

    (A) $1 + 4y$

    (B) $4y$

    (C) $1 + 2y$

    (D) $\dfrac{x+2y}{x}$

    (E) $\dfrac{x+3y}{x}$

2. Add $\dfrac{3c}{c+d} + \dfrac{3d}{c+d}$.

    (A) $\dfrac{6cd}{c+d}$

    (B) $\dfrac{3cd}{c+d}$

    (C) $\dfrac{3}{2}$

    (D) 3

    (E) $\dfrac{9cd}{c+d}$

3. Add $\dfrac{a}{5} + \dfrac{3a}{10}$.

    (A) $\dfrac{4a}{15}$

    (B) $\dfrac{a}{2}$

    (C) $\dfrac{3a^2}{50}$

    (D) $\dfrac{2a}{25}$

    (E) $\dfrac{3a^2}{15}$

4. Add $\dfrac{x+4}{6} + \dfrac{1}{2}$.

(A) $\dfrac{x+7}{6}$ (D) $\dfrac{x+5}{12}$

(B) $\dfrac{x+5}{8}$ (E) $\dfrac{x+5}{6}$

(C) $\dfrac{x+4}{12}$

5. Subtract $\dfrac{3b}{4} - \dfrac{7b}{10}$.

(A) $-\dfrac{2b}{3}$ (D) b

(B) $\dfrac{b}{5}$ (E) $\dfrac{2b}{3}$

(C) $\dfrac{b}{20}$

How wise? Check your answers on page 166.

Multiplication and Division

You'll see that this is all about factoring. Cancel out terms that are alike on top and bottom. Then multiply what's left. If those exponents scare you, remember the rule is to ADD them when you multiply and to SUBTRACT them when you divide.

Example: Find the product of $\dfrac{x^3}{y^2}$ and $\dfrac{y^3}{x^2}$.

Solution: x^2 can be canceled out on top and bottom, leaving one lonely x on top. Same with the y variables. You're left with $\dfrac{x}{1} \cdot \dfrac{y}{1}$. Multiply fractions and the answer is xy.

Example: Divide $\dfrac{15a^2b}{2}$ by $5a^3$.

Solution: Division is just multiplication by the multiplicative inverse:

$$\frac{15a^2b}{2} \cdot \frac{1}{5a^3}.$$

Cancel $5a^2$ on top and bottom, and you're left with $\dfrac{3b}{2} \cdot \dfrac{1}{a}$ or $\dfrac{3b}{2a}$.

I think you'll agree when we say these are more fun than real numbers. A b is a b, and you don't have to dig deeper to find its factors.

A b is a b, huh? Is that like "a rose is a rose"? Some English dude wrote that. So I guess math is as deep as English class.

Get Wise!
Multiply and divide the following problems.

1. Find the product of $\dfrac{x^2}{y^3}$ and $\dfrac{y^4}{x^5}$.

    (A) $\dfrac{y^2}{x^3}$ (D) $\dfrac{x^8}{y^7}$

    (B) $\dfrac{y}{x^3}$ (E) $\dfrac{x}{y}$

    (C) $\dfrac{x^3}{y}$

2. Multiply c by $\dfrac{b}{c}$.

(A) $\dfrac{b}{c^2}$

(D) c

(B) $\dfrac{c^2}{b}$

(E) bc^2

(C) b

3. Divide $\dfrac{ax}{by}$ by $\dfrac{x}{y}$.

(A) $\dfrac{ax^2}{by^2}$

(D) $\dfrac{by^2}{ax^2}$

(B) $\dfrac{b}{a}$

(E) $\dfrac{ay}{bx}$

(C) $\dfrac{a}{b}$

4. Divide $4abc$ by $\dfrac{2a^2b}{3d^2}$.

(A) $\dfrac{8a^3b^2c}{3d^2}$

(D) $\dfrac{6cd^2}{a}$

(B) $\dfrac{a}{6cd^2}$

(E) $\dfrac{5cd^2}{a}$

(C) $\dfrac{2ac}{bd^2}$

5. Divide $\dfrac{3a^2c^4}{4b^2}$ by $6ac^2$.

   (A) $\dfrac{ac^2}{8b^2}$ (D) $\dfrac{8b^2}{ac^2}$

   (B) $\dfrac{ac^2}{4b^2}$ (E) $\dfrac{ac^2}{6b^2}$

   (C) $\dfrac{4b^2}{ac^2}$

How wise? Check your answers on page 167.

COMPLEX FRACTIONS WITH VARIABLES

Complex algebraic fractions can look like monsters. But don't despair, they're simplified the same way you simplify complex fractions with no variables: Multiply *each term* of the entire complex fraction by the smallest item that will cancel out all denominators.

Example: Simplify $\dfrac{\dfrac{3}{x}+\dfrac{2}{y}}{6}$.

Solution: Since you have to get rid of those top fractions first, you multi-

ply *each term* by *xy:* $\dfrac{3y+2x}{6xy}$. And guess what? Stick a fork in;

you're done. Seriously. You can't cancel out terms or parts of terms. You don't know what those *x* and *y* variables really stand for! Leave them alone!

Get Wise!

Think you can stand the heat of the complex algebraic fractions? Then try these.

Get warmed up on one without variables:

1. Simplify $\dfrac{\dfrac{1}{5} - \dfrac{3}{2}}{\dfrac{3}{4}}$.

(A) $\dfrac{15}{26}$

(D) $\dfrac{26}{15}$

(B) $-\dfrac{15}{26}$

(E) $-\dfrac{26}{15}$

(C) 2

Now try some variables:

2. Simplify $\dfrac{\dfrac{a}{x^2}}{\dfrac{a^2}{x}}$.

(A) $\dfrac{x}{a}$

(D) ax

(B) $\dfrac{1}{a^2 x}$

(E) $\dfrac{a}{x}$

(C) $\dfrac{1}{ax}$

Now throw some addition and subtraction in there:

3. Simplify $\dfrac{\dfrac{1}{x}-\dfrac{1}{y}}{\dfrac{1}{x}+\dfrac{1}{y}}$.

(A) $\dfrac{x-y}{x+y}$ (D) -1

(B) $\dfrac{x+y}{x-y}$ (E) $-xy$

(C) $\dfrac{y-x}{x+y}$

Mix it up a bit:

4. Simplify $\dfrac{1+\dfrac{1}{x}}{\dfrac{1}{y}}$.

(A) $1+\dfrac{y}{x}$ (D) $\dfrac{y+1}{x}$

(B) $2y$ (E) $\dfrac{xy+1}{y}$

(C) $x+1$

And try your luck at exponents:

5. Simplify $\dfrac{2+\dfrac{t}{2}}{\dfrac{1}{t^2}}$.

   (A) $t^2 + t$ (D) $t + 1$

   (B) t^3 (E) $2+\dfrac{t}{2}$

   (C) $\dfrac{2t+1}{2}$

How wise? Check your answers on page 167.

OTHER USES FOR FACTORING

Stifle those wisecracks about where we can stick our factors. You should be happy to read that you know ALMOST everything you'll need to know about fractions in algebra for any basic math test. This last section is to prepare you for EVERY possible algebra situation. For example, what if you saw this:

Example: If $m^2 - n^2 = 48$ and $m + n = 12$, find $m - n$.

Solution: No, you won't skip it or bang your head in despair. You need to see that $m^2 - n^2$ is equal to $(m + n)(m - n)$. This is called the *difference of two squares*. They will ALWAYS be factored like that. Pretty cool, huh?

Now you know that these two quantities must multiply to 48. And the problem already tells you that one of them is 12! Easy, the other must be 4.

Notice that the problem doesn't care if you can solve for m or n! Don't do more work than is necessary. Who cares what m and n are? Here's another factoring fact:

Example: If $(a + b)^2 = 48$ and $ab = 6$, find $a^2 + b^2$.

Solution: The rule is that $(a + b)^2 = a^2 + 2ab + b^2$. No fancy name this time. Don't question it; memorize it. Now, how does the problem help us out from here? It tells us that ab is 6! Substitute that in and you get $a^2 + 2(6) + b^2 = 48$.

And we only have to solve for $a^2 + b^2$, not a, not b. Who cares! Subtract 12 from both sides: $a^2 + b^2 = 36$. Amazing! You *think* they're asking you to solve a complicated problem, but they really gave you all the answers!

Get Wise!

See if the problems below are within your level of understanding today. If not, try again tomorrow.

1. If $a + b = \dfrac{1}{3}$ and $a - b = \dfrac{1}{4}$, find $a^2 - b^2$. (Pssst, the difference of two squares, anyone?)

(A) $\dfrac{1}{12}$ (D) $\dfrac{1}{6}$

(B) $\dfrac{1}{7}$ (E) none of these

(C) $\dfrac{2}{7}$

2.   If $(a - b)^2 = 40$ and $ab = 8$, find $a^2 + b^2$.
 (A) 5   (D) 56
 (B) 24   (E) 32
 (C) 48

3.   If $a + b = 8$ and $a^2 - b^2 = 24$, then $a - b =$
 (A) 16   (D) 32
 (B) 4   (E) 6
 (C) 3

4.   The trinomial $x^2 + 4x - 45$ is exactly divisible by
 (A) $x + 9$ (D) $x + 15$
 (B) $x - 9$ (E) $x - 3$
 (C) $x + 5$

This next one looks trickier than it is. Concentrate.

5.   If $\dfrac{1}{c} - \dfrac{1}{d} = 5$ and $\dfrac{1}{c} + \dfrac{1}{d} = 3$, then $\dfrac{1}{c^2} - \dfrac{1}{d^2} =$
 (A) 16   (D) 15
 (B) 34   (E) cannot be determined
 (C) 2

How wise? Check your answers on page 168.

A Word to the Wise

Adding and Subtracting

★ Same denominator? Do the operation and put it over the denominator.

★ Different denominators? Find a common denominator or use the cross-multiplication trick that you learned in chapter 2.

Simplifying, Multiplying, and Dividing

* Factor out the *largest common factors* from quantities. Cancel them out in fractions.

* Use *FOIL* for trinomials: First, Outer, Inner, Last

* The *difference of two squares* is $m^2 - n^2 = (m + n)(m - n)$.

* To solve yucky-looking problems like "If $\dfrac{1}{p} - \dfrac{1}{s} = 2$ and $\dfrac{1}{p} + \dfrac{1}{s} = 3$,

  then $\dfrac{1}{p^2} - \dfrac{1}{s^2} = ?$" always look for trinomial factors or the difference of two squares.

* Only answer what you're *asked for*. You could waste your youth on impossibilities. If you need to find $\dfrac{1}{p^2} - \dfrac{1}{s^2}$, then don't stress out over what p or s equals!

* When dividing fractions, flip the second fraction and multiply.

Complex Fractions

* Just like complex fractions without variables, simplify these by multiplying *all* terms by the smallest item that cancels out all denominators.

ANSWERS TO CHAPTER 8: PRACTICE EXERCISES

Simplifying Algebraic Fractions (Page 151)

1. **(B)** $\dfrac{3x^2(x-y)}{9x(x-y)} = \dfrac{x}{3}$

2. **(A)** $\dfrac{2(x-4)}{3(4-x)} = -\dfrac{2}{3}$

3. **(E)** You know the denominator can't be 0. Trick: think of any fraction that looks like this, say $\dfrac{5-2}{2-5}$. It will ALWAYS equal (-1)!

4. **(C)** $\dfrac{(b+4)(b-3)}{(b+5)(b-3)} = \dfrac{(b+4)}{(b+5)}$

5. **(D)** $\dfrac{2(x+2y)}{6(x+2y)} = \dfrac{2}{6} = \dfrac{1}{3}$

Addition and Subtraction (Page 155)

1. **(D)** $\dfrac{6x+5y}{2x} - \dfrac{4x+y}{2x}$

    $= \dfrac{6x+5y-4x-y}{2x} = \dfrac{2x+4y}{2x}$

    $= \dfrac{2(x+2y)}{2x} = \dfrac{x+2y}{x}$

2. **(D)** $\dfrac{3c+3d}{c+d} = \dfrac{3(c+d)}{c+d} = 3$

3. **(B)** Multiply the first fraction by $\dfrac{2}{2}$, then add:

    $$\dfrac{2a+3a}{10} = \dfrac{5a}{10} = \dfrac{a}{2}$$

4. **(A)** Multiply the second fraction by $\dfrac{3}{3}$, then add:

    $\dfrac{x+4+3}{6} = \dfrac{x+7}{6}$

5. **(C)** $\dfrac{3b(10) - 4(7b)}{4(10)} = \dfrac{30b - 28b}{40}$

    $$= \dfrac{2b}{40} = \dfrac{b}{20}$$

Multiplication and Division (Page 157)

1. **(B)** Cancel out x^2 and y^3 on top and bottom: $\dfrac{y}{x^3}$.

2. **(C)** $c \cdot \dfrac{b}{c} = b$

3. **(C)** Multiply $\dfrac{ax}{by} \cdot \dfrac{y}{x}$. Cancel out y and x: $\dfrac{a}{b}$.

4. **(D)** Multiply $4abc \cdot \dfrac{3d^2}{2a^2b}$. Cancel out 2, a, and b (from ALL terms!):

$$2c \cdot \frac{3d^2}{a} = \frac{6cd^2}{a}$$

5. **(A)** Multiply $\dfrac{3a^2c^4}{4b^2} \cdot \dfrac{1}{6ac^2}$. Cancel out 3, a, and c^2:

$$\frac{ac^2}{4b^2} \cdot \frac{1}{2} = \frac{ac^2}{8b^2}$$

Complex Fractions with Variables (Page 160)

1. **(E)** Multiply every term by 20: $\dfrac{4-30}{15} = \dfrac{-26}{15}$

2. **(C)** Multiply every term by x^2: $\dfrac{a}{a^2x} = \dfrac{1}{ax}$

3. **(C)** Multiply every term by xy: $\dfrac{y-x}{y+x}$

4. **(A)** Multiply every term by xy: $1 + \dfrac{y}{x}$

5. **(E)** Multiply every term by t^2: $2 + \dfrac{t}{2}$

Other Uses for Factoring (Page 163)

1. **(A)** $(a+b)(a-b) = a^2 - b^2$

$$\left(\frac{1}{3}\right)\left(\frac{1}{4}\right) = a^2 - b^2$$

$$\frac{1}{12} = a^2 - b^2$$

Did you see that it's the difference of two squares?

2. **(D)** $(a-b)^2 = a^2 - 2ab + b^2 = 40$

Substituting 8 for *ab*:

$$a^2 - 16 + b^2 = 40$$

$$a^2 + b^2 = 56$$

3. **(C)** $(a+b)(a-b) = a^2 - b^2$

It's the difference of two squares. If we know $(a+b)$ is 8, then:

$$8(a-b) = 24$$

$$(a-b) = 3$$

4. **(A)** Factor that baby: $x^2 + 4x - 45 = (x+9)(x-5)$

5. **(D)** $\left(\frac{1}{c} - \frac{1}{d}\right)\left(\frac{1}{c} + \frac{1}{d}\right) = \frac{1}{c^2} - \frac{1}{d^2}$ What a mess! But look—the right side of the equal sign is the difference of two squares. That's all there is to it! Substitute (5) for the first quantity and (3) for the second and multiply $(5)(3) = \frac{1}{c^2} - \frac{1}{d^2}$. The answer is 15! And you thought you'd be here for hours . . .

chapter 9

Algebra

POSITIVITY AND NEGATIVITY

To play with numbers, you have to make sure you know how to work the signs.

Addition

If the signs are the same, add them and keep the sign. If the signs are different, subtract them and put the sign of the "bigger" number on the answer. "Bigger" in this case doesn't necessarily mean the number has the bigger value, just that it's the number with the higher value in a world where they're both positive.

Hold it. A world where everything is positive? Did I suddenly stumble into an episode of the "Brady Bunch"?

169

Example: Add the following:

+4	−4	−4	+4
+7	−7	+7	−7
+11	−11	+3	−3

See that last one? Surely −7 is smaller than 4; think of a number line. But a (7) is bigger than a (4) so the answer gets a negative sign!

Subtraction

Mind-blowing fact: Subtraction is really addition of the additive inverse. This means you don't have to learn another rule! To subtract, you only have to change the sign of the number you're subtracting and follow the addition rules above! And you thought this would be tough.

Example: Subtract the following:

+4	−4	−4	+4
−7	−7	−(−7)	−(−7)
−3	−11	3	11

Multiplication

A negative times a negative equals a positive. Don't question it, just know it. It's like in English when they tell you a double negative really means a positive: "I don't *not* understand this" means that you *do* understand. If the number of negative factors (numbers you're multiplying) is odd though, the negative sign sticks.

Example: Find the following products:

$$(+4)(+7) = +28 \qquad (+4)(−7) = −28$$

$$(−4)(−7) = +28 \qquad (−4)(+7) = −28$$

But: $(−4)(−7)(−1) = −28$ (Odd number of negative factors results in a negative answer.)

Division

Same signs equal a positive quotient. Different signs equal a negative quotient. (Remember, quotient in division means the answer.)

Example: Divide the following:

$$\frac{+28}{+4} = +7 \qquad \frac{-28}{+4} = -7$$

$$\frac{-28}{-4} = +7 \qquad \frac{+28}{-4} = -7$$

Division is usually so complicated. There are times when I wish division were as simple as when I, like, need to "divide" myself from a group of dorks in the lunch line or from my parents when we're on vacation.

Get Wise!

Add, subtract, multiply, divide, and conquer the sign problems below!

1. At 8 a.m. the temperature in Sunnydale was an unmanageable –4° F. If the temperature rose 7 degrees during the next hour, what was the temperature at 9 a.m.?
    (A) +11°
    (B) –11°
    (C) +7°
    (D) +3°
    (E) –3°

2. In Asia, the highest point is Mount Everest, with an altitude of 29,002 feet. The lowest point is the Dead Sea, at 1286 feet below sea level. What is the difference in their elevations?
    (A) 27,716 feet
    (B) 30,288 feet
    (C) 28,284 feet
    (D) 30,198 feet
    (E) 27,284 feet

3. Find the product of $(-6)(-4)(-4)$ and (-2).
   (A) -16 (D) $+192$
   (B) $+16$ (E) -98
   (C) -192

4. Temperatures were reported every hour during a brisk winter evening: $+4°$, $0°$, $-1°$, $-5°$, and $-8°$. Find the average temperature for these hours.

   (A) $-10°$ (D) $-2\frac{1}{2}°$
   (B) $-2°$ (E) $-3°$
   (C) $+2°$

5. Solve $5a - 4x - 3y$ if $a = -2$, $x = -10$, and $y = 5$.
   (A) $+15$ (D) -35
   (B) $+25$ (E) $+35$
   (C) -65

How wise? Check your answers on page 188.

LINEAR EQUATIONS

So you think you're ready for equations? Equations are used in algebra—a subject feared by many. We'll dive into algebra by stating the rules:

> **Rules. I knew I shouldn't trust this witty banter. How can equations have rules? They're just numbers and letters.**

1. Remove fractions or decimals using multiplication.

2. Remove parentheses by using the distributive law. (Check out Chapter 1 if this sounds as foreign as humburgenschtein.)

3. Isolate your variable (or whatever you're solving for) on one side of the equal sign. He will not be lonely; he will know he is almost solved.

WISE NOTE

Whenever a term crosses the equal sign from one side of the equation to the other, it must pay a toll. No, silly, you won't see a profit from this; rather, it must change its sign. Good news: There will be no Inflation.

4. Combine similar terms. In some algebra problems it's easiest if you do this a little beforehand, to get the equation ready for isolation of the variable. But it needs to be done in order to finish the problem.

5. Stuck? Try factoring if terms cannot be combined.

6. The final step is to divide by whatever number is stuck clinging to your variable. (This number is called the *coefficient* for those of you who want to use it to impress your friends).

Coefficients *is* a big word; however, I doubt my best friends Suzi and Mariana will be really impressed.

Example: Solve for *x:*

$$5x - 3 = 3x + 5 \quad \text{(Subtract } 3x \text{ from each side.)}$$
$$2x = 8 \quad \text{(Divide each side by 4.)}$$
$$x = 4$$

Example: Solve for *x:* $\dfrac{2}{3}x - 10 = \dfrac{1}{4}x + 15$

It's easiest if you first multiply by 12 to kill the fractions:

$$8x - 120 = 3x + 180$$
$$5x = 300$$
$$x = 60$$

Example: Solve for *x:* .3x + .15 = 1.65

Dislike decimals? We do. To ditch them, multiply by 100:

$$30x + 15 = 165$$
$$30x = 150$$
$$x = 5$$

And introducing . . . an equation with all variables!
Keep focused.

Example: Solve for *x: ax − r = bx − s*

Solution: $ax - bx = r - s$

$$x(a - b) = r - s$$

$$x = \frac{r - s}{a - b}$$

Same rules apply! Try it again.

Example: Solve for *x:* 6x − 2 = 8(x − 2)

Solution: $6x - 2 = 8x - 16$

$$14 = 2x$$

$$x = 7$$

Good. Now you're ready.

Get Wise!

The following problems will weed out the men from the boys and the women from the girls. Good luck!

1. Solve for *x:* 3x − 2 = 3 + 2x

    (A) 1   (D) 6

    (B) 5   (E) −5

    (C) −1

2. Solve for *a:* $8 - 4(a - 1) = 2 + 3(4 - a)$

    (A) $-\dfrac{5}{3}$ (D) -2

    (B) $-\dfrac{7}{3}$ (E) 2

    (C) 1

3. Solve for *x:* $\dfrac{1}{8}y + 6 = \dfrac{1}{4}y$

    (A) 48   (D) 1
    (B) 14   (E) 2
    (C) 6

4. Solve for *x:* $.02(x - 2) = 1$
    (A) 2.5   (D) 51
    (B) 52   (E) 6
    (C) 1.5

5. Solve for *x.* $4(x - r) = 2x + 10r$
    (A) $7r$ (D) $5.5r$

    (B) $3r$ (E) $2\dfrac{1}{3}r$

    (C) r

How wise? Check your answers on page 189.

SIMULTANEOUS EQUATIONS

Funny thing about equations: No matter what you multiply them by, they still keep the essence they were born with. Kind of like a DNA strand of genetic code. Don't think you care? Well, you should because this is GREAT news for anyone who has looked at a pair of equations and said, "Huh?" You probably didn't realize how much you could play with them.

The goal in solving a pair of equations for their unknown variables (usually x and y) is elimination of one of the unknowns. This way you have an equation with one unknown and you can solve it by using all the stuff you learned in the last section. (Provided that you actually read it!)

To eliminate an unknown, you can multiply one or both equations by a number that will rid you of a pesky variable term. You have to think one step ahead first and figure out if you want to add the equations or subtract them. (Yes! You can do that, too!)

I have a few pesky items I'd like to get rid of, but I don't think adding or subtracting will help!

Example: Solve for x: $7x + 5y = 15$
$$5x - 9y = 17$$

Solution: Since you're asked to solve for x, let's get rid of that silly y term. Since one y is positive and one is negative, we know that later we'll want to add the equations together to cancel them out. First, we need to make them have equal coefficients.

Multiply the first equation by 9:

$63x + 45y = 135$

Multiply the second by 5:

$25x - 45y = 85$

Sweet, your y terms now have opposite signs and can be eliminated by adding the two equations. By the way, if they had the *same* signs, we would eliminate by *subtracting* the two equations.

Adding, we have: $63x + 45y = 135$
$$25x - 45y = 85$$
$$88x = 220$$
$$x = 2\frac{1}{2}$$

We know you weren't asked to solve for y, but do you think you can do it? We'll give you two minutes to figure it out. OK, we lied, we'll tell you. Plug in 2.5 for x! (Decimals are easier than fractions, right?) Ready, set, go!

$$7(2.5) + 5y = 15$$
$$17.5 + 5y = 15$$
$$5y = -2.5$$
$$y = -.5 \ or -\frac{1}{2}$$

Congratulations (we hope). Let's try one with all variables.

Example: Solve for x: $ax + by = r$
$$cx - dy = s$$

Solution: Same as above, really. Multiply the first equation by d and the second by b to eliminate the y terms by addition.

$$adx + bdy = dr$$
$$bcx - bdy = bs$$
$$adx + bcx = dr + bs$$

That looks messy. But keep your goal in focus. What is x? Pull the x out of the two terms on the left (this is the infamous "factoring"):
$$x(ad + bc) = dr + bs$$

And make your x stand alone by dividing away that messy quantity in parentheses.

$$x(ad + bc) = dr + bs$$
$$x = \frac{dr + bs}{ad + bc}$$

Get Wise!

Let's do this. Solve the simultaneous equations.

1. Solve for x: $x - 3y = 3$
$$2x + 9y = 11$$

(A) 2   (D) 5
(B) 3   (E) 6
(C) 4

2. Solve for x: $.6x + .2y = 2.2$
$$.5x - .2y = 1.1$$

(A) 1   (D) 10
(B) 3   (E) 11
(C) 30

3. Solve for y: $2x + 3y = 12b$
$$3x - y = 7b$$

(A) $7\frac{1}{7}b$ (D) $1\frac{2}{7}$
(B) $2b$ (E) $-b$
(C) $3b$

4. If $2x = 3y$ and $5x + y = 34$, find y.

(A) 4   (D) 6.5
(B) 5   (E) 10
(C) 6

5. If $x + y = -1$ and $x - y = 3$, find y.

(A) 1   (D) 2
(B) -2   (E) 0
(C) -1

How wise? Check your answers on page 189.

QUADRATIC EQUATIONS

Probably the most feared of all the algebra equations, in corner number one, introducing, Quincy "The Quick" Quadratic! Applause, applause, applause. But seriously, quadratics stink not only because they're difficult to pronounce but also because the variable appears on two levels. And the solution to quadratic equations always has two roots, even though these roots may be equal. I know, it sounds like mumbo jumbo, but it looks like this: $ax^2 + bx + c = 0$, where a, b, and c are integers.

We'll make it so $ax^2 + bx + c$ can always be factored. It won't always work out this way, but we want you to understand the basics.

Anyway, if b and/or c is equal to 0, we have an incomplete quadratic equation. Don't worry—it can still be solved by factoring and will still have two roots.

Quadratics? Does that have something to do with 4 or water? What have I gotten myself into with this algebra? I need baby steps here!

Example: $x^2 + 5x = 0$

Solution: Factor out an x: $x(x + 5) = 0$.

Now, figure out what makes the equation true. Let's see, if x is 0, then 0 times the quantity will give you 0 (check). And if the quantity equals 0, which will happen if $x = -5$, then we'll still get 0. Your two roots (answers) are $x = \{0, -5\}$. Try another.

Example: $6x^2 - 8x = 0$

Solution: Factor out $2x$: $2x(3x - 4) = 0$.

Easiest way to finish? Set each factor equal to 0 and solve the new linear equations for x.

$$3x - 4 = 0$$
$$2x = 0 \qquad 3x = 4$$
$$x = 0 \qquad x = \frac{4}{3}$$

The roots (answers) of the quadratic are $\{0, \frac{4}{3}\}$.

Don't be fooled on this next one. This is where the test makers try to get you.

Example: $x^2 - 9 = 0$

Solution: Easy enough, right? $x^2 = 9$, so $x = 3$. But hold your horses there, cowboy! There are two answers. If a negative times a negative is a positive (and we learned that on the first page of this chapter) then wouldn't the answers be $\{3, -3\}$? Now you're talking.

Example: $x^2 - 8 = 0$

Solution: Uh oh, you know your simple squares, and 8 is NOT one of them. No worries. Just write it like this:

$$x^2 = 8$$
$$x = \pm\sqrt{8}$$

Simplify the radical to $\sqrt{4} \cdot \sqrt{2}$, or $x = \pm\, 2\sqrt{2}$.

Example: $16x^2 - 25 = 0$

Solution: This is factored with the principal of FOIL.

WISE NOTE

FOIL is a multiplication memorization trick that means:

<u>F</u>IRST

<u>O</u>UTER

<u>I</u>NNER

<u>L</u>AST

This is the order in which you multiply the equations:

$$(4x - 5)(4x + 5) = 16x^2 + 20x - 20x - 25$$

All this does is FOIL my plans for the evening. I'll be glad when I'm done studying.

As you see, the middle terms cancel out and you're left with the example above: $16x^2 - 25 = 0$

Don't be freaked out if you didn't see that at first glance. You must look at these problems as though they are products of two mini equations. Now to finish this example in this century:

Set each factor $(4x - 5)(4x + 5)$ equal to 0 and $x = \pm\dfrac{5}{4}$.

If you wanted to solve this without factoring, you would get:

$$16x^2 = 25$$

$$x^2 = \frac{25}{16}$$

$$x = \pm\frac{5}{4}$$

Same answer, different technique. Math's all about that. Now try a problem with a *middle term*.

Example: $x^2 + 6x + 8 = 0$

Solution: We know that the two last numbers will multiply together to get 8 so we have either: (? + 4)(? + 2) or (? + 8)(? +1). The question here is not about the first term, since it is only an x times an x. The question is *how can you get the middle term to add up to 6x?* This is how: $(x + 2)(x + 4) = 0$

Set each factor equal to 0 and you get $x = -4$ or $x = -2$.

One more step to learn—you're doing great!

Example: $x^2 - 2x - 15 = 0$

Solution: Now you need two numbers that multiply to get –15. *Hint:* They must have opposite signs since your "L" in FOIL is negative. To get –2 as a middle term, the numbers must be –5 and +3.
$$(x - 5)(x + 3) = 0$$

And the roots are $\{5, -3\}$.

Get Wise!

The quadratic equations below will challenge and charm, we're sure.

1. Solve for x: $x^2 - 8x - 20 = 0$
    (A) 5 or –4   (D) –10 or –2
    (B) 10 or –2   (E) –10 or 2
    (C) –5 or 4

2. Solve for x: $25x^2 - 4 = 0$

    (A) $\dfrac{4}{25}$ or $-\dfrac{4}{25}$ (D) $-\dfrac{2}{5}$ only

    (B) $\dfrac{2}{5}$ or $-\dfrac{2}{5}$ (E) none of these

    (C) $\dfrac{2}{5}$ only

3. Solve for x: $6x^2 - 42x = 0$

(A) 7 only   (D) 7 or 0

(B) −7 only   (E) −7 or 0

(C) 0 only

4. Solve for x: $x^2 - 19x + 48 = 0$

(A) 8 or 6   (D) 12 or 4

(B) 24 or 2   (E) none of these

(C) −16 or −3

5. Solve for x: $3x^2 = 81$

(A) $9\sqrt{3}$ (D) $\pm 3\sqrt{3}$

(B) $\pm 9\sqrt{3}$ (E) ± 9

(C) $3\sqrt{3}$

How wise? Check your answers on page 191.

RADICALS RULE

Radicals may be fun to say, but they need to be isolated in equations like hardened criminals. You get rid of them by squaring both sides. This can be tricky—the ENTIRE side gets squared, not each term. Let's look at some:

Example: $\sqrt{5-52} + 63\sqrt[3]{2} = 569,800$

You know how to proceed, right? Isolate the radical. If you've been paying attention, you'll see . . . well, that this was a trick. There can be no negative numbers under the radical signs. Forgive us.

Squares, criminals, radicals, isolation . . . Is this some kind of spy movie to scare us or is it algebra?

Example: $\sqrt{x-3} = 4$

Solution: Yup, sorry. This one's for real.

So square both sides: $(\sqrt{x-3})^2 = 4^2$

And solve for x: $x - 3 = 16$

$$x = 19$$

Check your math: $\sqrt{16} = 4$, true!

Example: $\sqrt{x-3} = -4$

Solution: Square both sides: $x - 3 = 16$

$$x = 19$$

Check your math: $\sqrt{16} = -4$, not true.

This equation has no solution because when you get an answer from underneath a radical sign, it can only be positive. Pretty cool, huh? The right answer is "no answer."

Example: $\sqrt{x^2 - 7} + 1 = x$

Solution: First, get the radical alone on one side, then square:

$$\sqrt{x^2 - 7} = x - 1$$
$$x^2 - 7 = x^2 - 2x + 1$$
$$-7 = -2x + 1$$
$$2x = 8$$
$$x = 4$$

Remember to square ENTIRE sides, not individual pieces of each. It doesn't work out any other way. Check your math:

$$\sqrt{4^2 - 7} + 1 = 4$$
$$\sqrt{9} + 1 = 4$$
$$3 + 1 = 4 \quad \text{True!}$$

Get Wise!

The last practice section, we promise. Do your best and be rewarded by our next chapter.

1. Solve for *y:* $\sqrt{2y} + 11 = 15$

   (A) 4   (D) 1
   (B) 2   (E) no solution
   (C) 8

Are you checking your answers?

2. Solve for *x:* $4\sqrt{2x-1} = 12$

   (A) 18.5   (D) 5
   (B) 4   (E) no solution
   (C) 10

3. Solve for *x:* $\sqrt{x^2 - 35} = 5 - x$

   (A) 6   (D) −3
   (B) −6   (E) no solution
   (C) 3

Still checking your answers?

4. Solve for *y:* $26 = 3\sqrt{2y} + 8$

   (A) 6   (D) −6
   (B) 18   (E) no solution
   (C) 3

5. Solve for *x:* $\sqrt{\dfrac{2x}{5}} = 4$

   (A) 10   (D) 40
   (B) 20   (E) no solution
   (C) 30

How about that last one? Still checking? I know I am!

How wise? Check your answers on page 192.

A Word to the Wise

We're really proud of the fact that you're finally on this page. Your hard work shows your dedication to learning all that we've taught. Now you're here to review all you've learned and take it all in one last time for final digestion. Give yourself a pat on the back for a job well done! (Of course, that was meant to make you feel guilty if you skipped the chapter and went here first in search of a quick fix. Did it work?)

Positive and Negative Numbers

* To *add* a *positive* and a *negative*, subtract and take the sign of the number farthest from zero on a number line.

* To *add two negatives*, just add and put a negative sign on the answer.

* Instead of subtracting, you'll want to *add the opposite*. Follow rules for addition.

* In multiplication, remember *two negatives make a positive*. One of each makes a negative.

* In division, if the signs are the *same,* it's a positive answer. If the signs are *different*, it's a negative answer.

Linear Equations

* The goal is to isolate the variable.

★ The obstacles are:

1. Fractions/Decimals—get rid of them by *multiplying*

2. Parentheses—follow rules of *distribution*

3. Dissimilar terms—try to *factor*

4. Coefficients—*divide* both sides by it to clear

Simultaneous Equations

★ *Solving* for your *variable*:

1. Get rid of unneeded terms by adding or subtracting entire equations.

2. Solve like a linear equation.

★ *Reminder:* You can (and may have to) multiply entire equations by a number to help you cancel out a term.

Quadratic Equations

★ The Look: $ax^2 + bx + c = 0$

★ The Facts:

1. You get two answers, called *roots*.

2. You use FOIL to figure out the factoring equations.

Radicals

★ To get rid of radicals, *square both sides*—as whole sides, not just as individual pieces.

★ *Reminder:* Though $x^2 = 9$ has two answers, $x = 3$ and -3, the radical sign means that the root is always just positive. So $\sqrt{9} = 3$, and only 3.

The Chi Algebra Bribe: If I check my answers and find that I got at least 25 of 30 right, then I can treat myself to a guilt-free pint of mint chocolate chip. Now that's radical!

ANSWERS TO CHAPTER 9: PRACTICE EXERCISES

Positives and Negatives (Page 171)

1. **(D)** $(-4) + (+7) = +3$ Think of a number line!

2. **(B)** $(29,002) - (-1286) = 30,288$

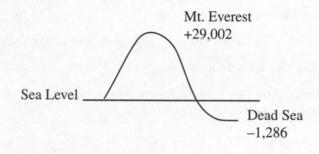

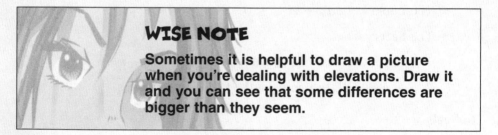

WISE NOTE

Sometimes it is helpful to draw a picture when you're dealing with elevations. Draw it and you can see that some differences are bigger than they seem.

3. **(D)** Two negatives equal a positive—Twice!

    $$6 \times 4 \times 4 \times 2 = 192$$

4. **(B)** Remember averages?

    $$\frac{+4+0+(-1)+(-5)+(-8)}{5} = \frac{-10}{5} = -2°$$

5. **(A)** Just substitution: $5(-2) - 4(-10) - 3(5) = -10 + 40 - 15 = +15$

Linear Equations (Page 174)

    1.   **(B)** $3x - 2 = 3 + 2x$

$$x = 5$$

    2.   **(D)** $8 - 4a + 4 = 2 + 12 - 3a$

$$12 - 4u = 14 - 3a$$

$$-2 = a$$

    3.   **(A)**   Did you multiply by 8 to clear the fractions?

$$y + 48 = 2y$$

$$48 = y$$

    4.   **(B)**   Did you multiply by 100 to clear the decimals?

$$2(x - 2) = 100$$

$$2x - 4 = 100$$

$$2x = 104$$

$$x = 52$$

    5.   **(A)** $4x - 4r = 2x + 10r$ Still with us? Good job!

$$2x = 14r$$

$$x = 7r$$

Simultaneous Equations (Page 178)

    1.   **(C)**   Multiply first equation by 3, then add them:

$$3x - 9y = 9$$
$$\underline{2x + 9y = 11}$$
$$5x = 20$$
$$x = 4$$

2. **(B)** Multiply each equation by 10, then add:

$$6x + 2y = 22$$
$$\underline{5x - 2y = 11}$$
$$11x = 33$$
$$x = 3$$

3. **(B)** Multiply the first equation by 3 and the second by 2, then subtract:

$$6x + 9y = 36b$$
$$\underline{6x - 2y = 14b}$$
$$11y = 22b$$
$$y = 2b$$

4. **(A)** Rewrite: $2x - 3y = 0$
$$5x + y = 34$$

Variables all on one side, please! Tried to trick you.

Multiply the first equation by 5, the second by 2, and subtract.

$$10x - 15y = 0$$
$$\underline{10x + 2y = 68}$$
$$-17y = -68$$
$$y = 4$$

5. **(B)** Subtract the equations. No multiplication is needed.

$$x + y = -1$$
$$\underline{x - y = 3}$$
$$2y = -4$$
$$y = -2$$

Quadratic Equations (Page 182)

1. **(B)** You have to get (-8) as the middle term.

$$(x - 10)(x + 2) = 0$$
$$x - 10 = 0 \quad x + 2 = 0$$
$$x = 10 \text{ or } -2$$

2. **(B)** $(5x - 2)(5x + 2) = 0$

$$5x - 2 = 0 \quad 5x + 2 = 0$$
$$x = \frac{2}{5} \text{ or } -\frac{2}{5}$$

You could also use this method: $25x^2 = 4$

$$x^2 = \frac{4}{25}$$

3. **(D)** $6x(x - 7) = 0$

$$6x = 0 \quad\quad x - 7 = 0$$
$$x = 0 \text{ or } 7$$

4. **(E)** $(x - 16)(x - 3) = 0$

$$x - 16 = 0 \quad x - 3 = 0$$
$$x = 16 \text{ or } 3$$

5. **(D)** Check this out!

Divide both sides by 3:

$$x^2 = 27$$

So $x = \pm\sqrt{27}$ AND you know that $\sqrt{27} = \sqrt{9} \cdot \sqrt{3} = 3\sqrt{3}$.

To be complete, you must write $x = \pm3\sqrt{3}$.

Radicals (Page 185)

1. **(C)** $\sqrt{2y} = 4$

$2y = 16$

$y = 8$

Remember to check: $\sqrt{16} = 4$, true.

2. **(D)** $4\sqrt{2x-1} = 12$

$\sqrt{2x-1} = 3$

$2x - 1 = 9$

$2x = 10$

$x = 5$

Check: $4\sqrt{9} = 12$, true.

3. **(E)** $x^2 - 35 = 25 - 10x + x^2$

$-35 = 25 - 10x$

$10x = 60$

$x = 6$

Check: $\sqrt{1} = 5 - 6$, not true.

4. **(B)** $18 = 3\sqrt{2y}$

$6 = \sqrt{2y}$

$36 = 2y$

$y = 18$

Check: $26 = 3\sqrt{36} + 8$

$26 = 3(6) + 8$, true.

5. **(D)** $\dfrac{2x}{5} = 16$

$2x = 80$

$x = 40$

LAST ONE!!! Check: $\sqrt{\dfrac{80}{5}} = \sqrt{16} = 4$, TRUE! Don't you love it when they work out to be true?

chapter 10

Geometry

If the thought of circles and squares makes you want to give up math and seek comfort in daytime talk shows, don't despair. Although there are many concepts to be reviewed in geometry, the most basic ideas are just that—basic: lines, angles, and common shapes. Some tests, like the SAT, even give you the info you'll need in a small box at the beginning of each math section. Not all evil test makers expect you to be memorization gurus, they just want to see that you know what to do with the formulas.

Still shaking with fear and anxiety? How about a little background and real-world connections?

Can you imagine what life was like in 300 B.C.E.? No phones, computers, engines, plumbing . . . Now imagine the big questions that would plague you, like "What cave is most comfortable?" and "How big is this darn forest?" Some guy named Euclid wondered these very thoughts and decided to make a system called "geometry." *Geometry* literally means "measurement of the earth" in

195

Get Wise! Mastering Math Skills   *www.petersons.com*

Greek, so you can figure out what it was first used for. History class has surely taught you that ancient people had an unnatural obsession with maps.

The unique thing about geometry was that it provided a new way of thinking that wasn't all numbers and measurements. Today we use geometry in almost every line of work; the sciences especially wouldn't function without it. More specifically, pool sharks would be lost in angles and vectors, robotics would fall apart, roller coasters would be deemed national disaster sights, and carpenters would build houses that came with warnings. Not to mention there would be no computer animation!

So you see, geometry is the first math you encounter in school where you're asked to really think about the shapes of things. In geometry, something is either true or it isn't. You can't sway your teacher's decision by arguing louder. But the scary thing is, geometry makes you play with shapes and ideas *inside* your head.

And for some, the head is a lonely, open space with a circumference of 18 inches and an area of 16π. See? I do know geometry.

Ready to learn geometry? Let's begin. And remember, the only angle from which to approach a problem is the "Try Angle."

THE LINE

We'll start you off at the beginning. The simple line. Admire its shape and lack of bumps and curves:

The rule of a line is that it equals 180°. Any two angles next to each other on a line will add up to 180°.

Example: Find the measure of angle 2:

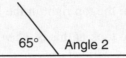

65° \ Angle 2

Solution: Since the measure of $\angle 1 = 65°$ and both must add up to 180°, then the measure of $\angle 2$ is $180° - 65°$, or 115°.

Parallel Lines

When you lined up for lunch in second grade, your teacher may have asked for two lines: one line for the boys and one for the girls. These lines were meant to be *parallel* (but rarely ever were), which means they never touch for as long as they go on in space.

> **Other things that should never touch: forks to peas, my brother and my CDs, or any other girl and my boyfriend.**

Parallel lines have another special quality if a line cuts through them.

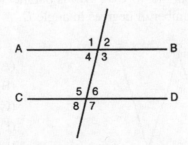

In the picture above, If $\overline{AB}$ is parallel to $\overline{CD}$, then:

$\angle 1 = \angle 3$, $\angle 5$, and $\angle 7$
$\angle 2 = \angle 4$, $\angle 6$, and $\angle 8$

Some textbooks will say they're *congruent*, but that just means equal. You should notice that all the opposite angles are equal AND the top and bottom clusters of four angles are identical. So the angle on the top right in the top cluster equals the angle in the top right in the bottom cluster.

Another easy way to look at this is *when parallel lines are cut by another line, all big angles formed are equal and all little angles formed are equal.*

Tips to remember when solving these types of problems:

1. *Extend your lines.* When you're told that two lines are parallel, make them bigger so you can see where they are crossed and how the angles look.

2. *Write down ALL the info you know.* Attack your problem with knowledge. Fill in numbers for opposite angles and angles next to each other on a line immediately.

3. *Terminology:* A *bisector* will cut any angle, line, or shape into two EQUAL parts. "Bi" means "two," and sector is part of the word "intersect."

Get Wise!

Try the line problems below so we can move on to shapes!

1. If $\overline{AB}$ is parallel to $\overline{CD}$, $\overline{BC}$ is parallel to $\overline{ED}$, and angle $B = 30°$, find the number of degrees in angle D.

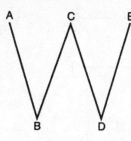

(A) 30
(B) 60
(C) 150
(D) 120
(E) none of these

2. If $\overline{AB}$ is parallel to $\overline{CD}$, angle $A = 35°$, and angle $C = 45°$, find the number of degrees in angle AEC ("angle AEC" is another way of saying angle E).

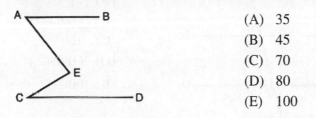

(A) 35
(B) 45
(C) 70
(D) 80
(E) 100

3. If $\overline{AB}$ is parallel to $\overline{CD}$ and angle 1 = 130°, find angle 2.

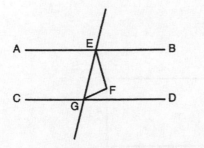

(A) 130°
(B) 100°
(C) 40°
(D) 60°
(E) 50°

4. If $\overline{AB}$ is parallel to $\overline{CD}$, $\overline{EF}$ bisects angle BEG, and $\overline{GF}$ bisects angle EGD, find the number of degrees in angle EFG.

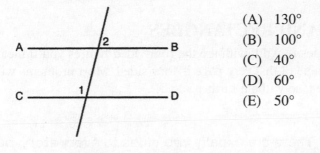

(A) 40
(B) 60
(C) 90
(D) 120
(E) cannot be determined

5. If $\overline{AB}$ is parallel to $\overline{CD}$ and angle 1 = $x°$, then the sum of angle 1 and angle 2 is

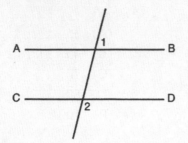

(A) $2x°$
(B) $(180 - x)°$
(C) $180°$
(D) $(180 + x)°$
(E) none of these

How wise? Check your answers on page 227.

SQUARES AND RECTANGLES

The easiest shapes to work with are the four-sided figures you'll meet here. After all, the shape of this very page is four-sided. Most problems will ask for perimeter or area, so without further ado . . .

There are usually two sides to every story, but these shapes have four! I can imagine that a disagreement between Sponge Bob Square Pants and his relatives must be rather confusing!

Rectangles

A *rectangle* looks like this:

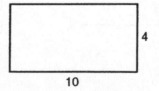

To find the *perimeter*, you add up the sides. (Notice how opposite sides are equal? That's what makes it a rectangle!)

$$P = l + l + w + w = 2l + 2w = 2(10) + 2(4) = 20 + 8 = 28$$

To find the *area*, you multiply the two sides next to each other: length × width.

$$A = l \times w = 10 \times 4 = 40$$

Each angle in a rectangle is 90°, and they add up to 360°.

Squares

A *square* has four equal sides and looks like this:

To find the *perimeter*, multiply one side by 4. That's the same as saying add up the sides because they're all equal.

$$P = 4 \times s = 4s = 4 \times 5 = 20$$

To find the *area*, just square one side. That's the same as length × width.

$$A = s^2 = 5^2 = 25$$

Like rectangles, each angle in a square is 90°, and they add up to 360°.

Get Wise!

Practice some problems on the area and perimeter of squares and rectangles. Remember to draw pictures to help you. Geometry is art with math!

1. The dimensions of a rectangular living room are 18 feet by 20 feet. How many square yards of carpeting are needed to cover the floor?
    (A) 360
    (B) 42
    (C) 40
    (D) 240
    (E) 90

2. A square has a side with length s. What is the area minus the perimeter?

    (A) $s^2 - 4s$ (D) $-4s$

    (B) s^2 (E) $s^2 - s$

    (C) $2s - s$

3. A square is equal in area to a rectangle with a width of 9 and height of 4. Find the perimeter of the square.

    (A) 36   (D) 24

    (B) 26   (E) none of these

    (C) 13

4. If the length and width of a rectangle are each doubled, the new area is what percent of the original?

    (A) 50%   (D) 300%

    (B) 100%   (E) 400%

    (C) 200%

How wise? Check your answers on page 229.

TRIANGLES

A triangle comes in many forms. Yes, they all have three sides and three angles (hence, the name **tri**angle), but there are mysteries lurking within their three walls. The following basics apply to all triangles:

To find the *perimeter* of a triangle, add up its sides.

Example:

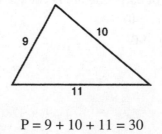

$$P = 9 + 10 + 11 = 30$$

To find the *area* of a triangle, use the formula $\frac{1}{2}bh$ where b is base and h is height.

Example:

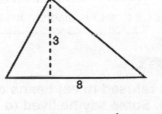

$$A = \frac{1}{2}(8 \cdot 3) = 12$$

When my little brother was born, we had to move to a house with a bigger *area*. That just gave him more room to run around in and annoy me.

The measures of all the angles in a triangle add up to 180°.

Make a habit of filling in all the info you can find in a problem, like the missing angle in the problem below. The key is to attack. Good defense never scored any runs.

Example:

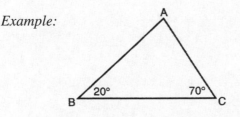

Since angles $A + B + C = 180°$, the missing angle in the triangle above is $180 - 90$, or 90°.

One more fun fact that holds true for all triangles: If opposite angles are equal, so are the opposite sides, and vice versa.

Right Triangles

If a triangle has a little box in one corner, then the angle is a right angle and has 90°. Right triangles make life easy because of Pythagoras. Pythagoras was a guy who lived way before Euclid wrote down geometry. As a matter of fact, Pythagoras lived so long ago that he couldn't even write on paper or trees like other early dudes; he had to use a tablet to set his theorem in stone, so to speak.

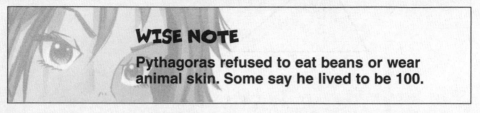

WISE NOTE
Pythagoras refused to eat beans or wear animal skin. Some say he lived to be 100.

Pythagoras figured out that there was a relationship between the sides in a right triangle. Yes, he had a lot of time on his hands while he was a prisoner of war in Babylon.

Pythagoras's Theorem is written as: $a^2 + b^2 = c^2$ where a and b are the smaller sides and c is the hypotenuse (long term for the long side of a right triangle). The Pythagorean theorem helps solve problems like these:

Example: For the following right triangle, find the value of x.

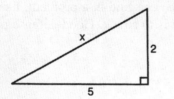

Solution:
$$\left(5\right)^2 + \left(2\right)^2 = x^2$$
$$25 + 4 = x^2$$
$$29 = x^2$$
$$x = \sqrt{29}$$

Not too hard, right? Don't worry, there will be plenty of practice on this soon. First, we must look at some special triangles.

Special Right Triangles

⋆ *Pythagorean Triples*

Luckily, in right triangles, certain side lengths can only go with other lengths. The 90° angle in the corner puts a magic spell on the lengths. The most common ones are:

3 , 4 , 5—and doubled 6 , 8 , 10

5, 12, 13—and doubled 10 , 24 , 26

8, 15, 17

Why is this lucky, you may ask? Well, if you see a right triangle in a problem with two side lengths that match these numbers, your work is done. We call them *Pythagorean Triples*. You'll be able to fill in the third side with no funny math business.

⋆ *Third Side Rule*

This is conceptual, so bear with us. Each side of a triangle is smaller in length to the sum of the other two sides. You could write the rule like this: Close your eyes and imagine a straight line. Now put another line of the same length above it. Grab the middle of the top line and pull it up so the two lines form a triangle. Notice that the higher you pull the top line, the more is left over on the sides of the bottom line that are NOT sides of your triangle.

Take a look at triangle *ABC*:

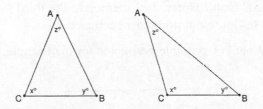

Notice that their shapes are quite different from each other—both in terms of angle sizes and side lengths. Each side of a triangle is smaller in length than the sum of the lengths of the other two sides; for example:

$$\overline{AC} < \overline{AB} + \overline{BC}$$
$$\overline{BC} < \overline{AB} + \overline{AC}$$
$$\overline{AB} < \overline{BC} + \overline{AC}$$

This makes good sense if you stop for a minute and think about it. What if two sides added together equaled a third side in length? The triangle would collapse, wouldn't it? You'd end up with overlapping parts, and that would be a sad excuse for a triangle!

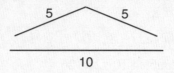

See, you can push those sides down and down until they become straight. Alas, you will still have no triangle. Just two parallel lines!

So, the *Third Side Rule* shows that **the third side cannot be *smaller* than the *difference* of the other two sides**. That means if you subtract two side lengths, the third side must be larger than that difference.

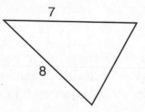

In the picture above, you can see that if the third side were a length of 1 or 2, the two sides of the triangle wouldn't touch! It wouldn't be big enough to get the two sides together to form a triangle.

Still confused? Don't worry. Just memorize the third side rule and move on. You'll need it to figure out problems such as this:

Example: What is a possible perimeter for the triangle below?

You know that the third side must be greater than 1 (and it does look to be that!) and smaller than 15. Choose any number between 1 and 15 and find your perimeter.

$7 + 8 + (10) = 25$. The perimeter can be written as: $16 < P < 30$

WISE NOTE

OK, so what did that all mean in one sentence or less? Rule: The third side of a triangle can never be greater than the sum or smaller than the difference of the other two sides. So there!

Altitudes and Equilaterals

The height, or *altitude*, of a triangle is an important measurement. Height is necessary to find the area or to calculate missing side lengths. In most triangles like the one below, you'll be given the height.

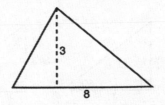

Otherwise, there would be no easy way to find it! And by the way, if you're having difficulty finding the altitude, look at other facts in the problem. More than likely there is a special right triangle or other shape that you have overlooked!

Then there are *equilateral* triangles. The name suggests that equality is lurking in there and that is absolutely the case. Not only are all sides equal, but also the measure of each angle in the triangle equals 60°. You can actually find the measurement of the altitude in an equilateral triangle with the formula

$\frac{1}{2}$ side $\cdot \sqrt{3}$.

Example: What is the altitude of the following triangle?

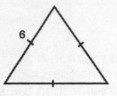

Solution: Altitude: $\frac{1}{2}$ side $\cdot \sqrt{3} = 3\sqrt{3}$

30–60–90 Triangles

The rules of a 30–60–90 triangle are:

★ The side opposite the 30° angle is half the hypotenuse.

★ The side opposite the 60° angle is half the hypotenuse times $\sqrt{3}$.

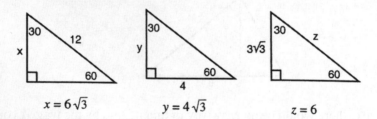

45–45–90 Triangles

The rules of a 45–45–90 triangle are:

★ Each side is half the hypotenuse times $\sqrt{2}$.

★ The hypotenuse is a leg times $\sqrt{2}$.

★ The diagonal of a square forms a 45–45–90 triangle and is therefore equal to a side times $\sqrt{2}$.

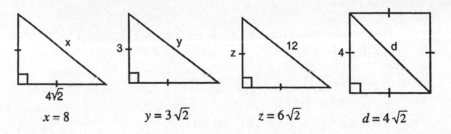

$x = 8$ $y = 3\sqrt{2}$ $z = 6\sqrt{2}$ $d = 4\sqrt{2}$

Similar Triangles

Two triangles are said to be similar if the angles are the same and the sides are in proportion. In the triangles below, the measure of angle B equals the measure of angle E and the measure of angle C equals the measure of angle F. Proportions (which, you'll remember, can be written as fractions) will help you here.

Example: What is x in the two similar triangles below?

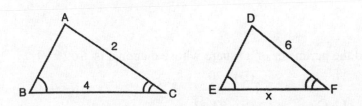

Solution: To find x, first find the relationship between the two triangles. The ratio of the known sides is 2:6 (or to make it simple, 1:3). That means the other sides must also be in that proportion: 4:12. Therefore, x is 12.

For a shape with only three sides, triangles have so much to remember! Move over, Euclid, I'm gonna start my own new school of geometry. No triangles allowed!

Get Wise!

Figure out the following triangle problems. Hope you paid attention and don't forget to *draw pictures!*

1. In triangle ABC, $AB = BC$, angle B contains x degrees. Find the number of degrees in angle A.

    (A) x (D) $90 - \dfrac{x}{2}$

    (B) $180 - x$ (E) $90 - x$

    (C) $180 - \dfrac{x}{2}$

2. Two boats leave the same dock at the same time, one traveling due west at 8 miles per hour and the other due north at 15 miles per hour. How many miles apart are the boats after three hours? (Draw a triangle!)

    (A) 17   (D) 51
    (B) 69   (E) 39
    (C) 75

3. Find the perimeter of a square whose diagonal is $6\sqrt{2}$.

    (A) 24   (D) 20

    (B) $12\sqrt{2}$ (E) $24\sqrt{2}$

    (C) 12

4. Find the length of $\overline{DB}$.

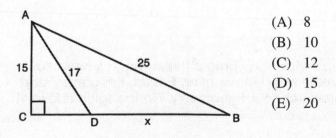

    (A) 8
    (B) 10
    (C) 12
    (D) 15
    (E) 20

5. In triangle *ABC*, the angles are in a ratio of 1:1:2. The largest angle of the triangle is

(A) 45° (D) 120°

(B) 60° (E) 100°

(C) 90°

How wise? Check your answers on page 229.

CIRCLES

Circles are the shapes of childhood: carousels, baseballs, ice cream scoops, wheels, and even bruises. Circles are also symbols of dreams and optimism— they have no end. Circles also come with new vocabulary.

> Sometimes my head spins around and around in circles when I try to digest too much geometry at one time. I'm going to go eat a pizza.

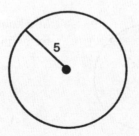

Look at the circle above. The line from the center to the edge is a *radius*. Here the radius is 5. Once you know the radius, you can calculate the perimeter and the area. Of course, to do that you should first know about *pi*. The symbol for pi is π and it is an irrational number. That means it is an approximation and should be written as a symbol unless you're told otherwise. It is equal to about

3.14159265, or $\dfrac{22}{7}$, if you're the type who needs to know. Let's enjoy some pi, shall we?

The perimeter of a circle is called its *circumference* (C) and the formula is $C = \pi d$. The *d* stands for diameter, which is nothing more than twice the radius. A diameter cuts the circle into two equal pieces because it always goes through the center.

Example: Find the circumference of the circle below.

Solution: $C = \pi d = 10\pi$

Great, now what about *area* (A), you ask? The area of a circle is $A = \pi r^2$ where *r* is the radius

Example: Find the area of the circle in the first example.

Solution: $A = \pi r^2 = 25\pi$

Once you know any one of these four—radius (*r*), diameter (*d*), circumference (*C*), or area (*A*)—you can calculate the other three. Try some examples.

Example:

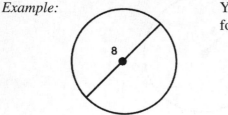

You know the diameter is 8. Find the following:

$r =$ ____

$C =$ ____

$A =$ ____

Solution: If you worked out the proper formulas, you should have written: radius = 4, $C = \pi \cdot 8 = 8\pi$, and A = 16π.

Example: Here's a trickier one. What if you only have the area?

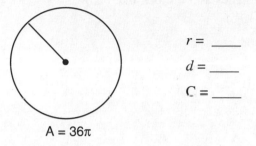

$r =$ ____
$d =$ ____
$C =$ ____

$A = 36\pi$

Solution: If you wrote that the radius is 6, the diameter is 12, and the circumference is 12π, then you are catching on.

By the way, any problem that deals with wheel revolutions is a circle question. Think of a wheel spinning; a full time around is one revolution and it would travel the length of one circumference as if laid out in a straight line!

And wheels simply make life more meaningful. At least that's what I keep telling my parents.

Example: Find the distance covered by this wheel in one revolution.

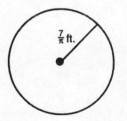

$\frac{7}{\pi}$ ft.

Solution: Find the circumference: $2 \cdot \pi \cdot \dfrac{7}{\pi} = 14$ feet. Pretty easy.

All angles in a circle add up to 360°. Think of a clock. Suppose an angle was formed by the big and little hands at 3 o'clock like below:

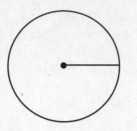

The hands form a 90° angle. You can see that four of them would go around the whole circle. Mathematically, 90 × 4 = 360. Angles in circle problems are often asked in relation to clocks. Remember, there are 12 numbers on a clock, so the proportion to degrees is $\frac{360}{12} = \frac{30}{1}$. This means there is 30° between each number in the circle.

Get Wise!

Decipher the mysteries of the circle in the following problems.

1. A circle has radius x. The area of the circle is 4. Find the area of a circle whose radius is $3x$. (It's easy to do this problem in two steps; first solve for x!)

    (A) 12   (D) 48

    (B) 36   (E) 144

    (C) $4\sqrt{3}$

2. A circle below is contained in a square whose side is 6. What is the area of the circle?

    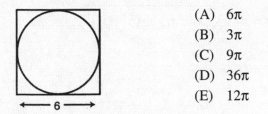

    (A) 6π

    (B) 3π

    (C) 9π

    (D) 36π

    (E) 12π

3. If the radius of a circle is increased by 3, the circumference is increased by

    (A) 3   (D) 6π

    (B) 3π (E) 4.5

    (C) 6

4. The hour hand of a clock is 3 feet long. How many feet does the tip of this hand move between 9:30 p.m. and 1:30 a.m. the following day?

    (A) π (D) 4π

    (B) 2π (E) 24π

    (C) 3π

5. The radius of a wheel is 18 inches. Find the number of feet covered by this wheel in 20 revolutions.

    (A) 360π (D) 720

    (B) 360   (E) 60π

    (C) 720π

How wise? Check your answers on page 231.

COORDINATE PLANES

It might sound unfamiliar but have you ever been asked to plot a point? Coordinate geometry is used in business, history, economics, computer graphics, and other areas where there are relationships between points. Don't worry—we're just going to be concerned with the math questions here. In math you'll need to know about three major point-plotting concepts: distance, slope, and midpoint. Just as you suspected, there are formulas for each. The formulas are going to look much worse than they really are. But it's easy! You just plug in points for the x and y variables.

Distance

The formula for distance is $D = \sqrt{\left(x_2 - x_1\right)^2 + \left(y_2 - y_1\right)^2}$.

Another formula? Before I read this book, I thought formula was for babies!

Example: Find the distance from point A with coordinates of (4,3) to point B with coordinates (8,6).

Solution: No need to draw your lines and plot your points. Remember, coordinates are always written in the form (x,y) and NOT the other way around. The x is plotted along the horizontal line in your plane. Plug your points into the formula for distance:

$$D = \sqrt{\left(8 - 4\right)^2 + \left(6 - 3\right)^2} = \sqrt{4^2 + 3^2} = \sqrt{16 + 9} = \sqrt{25} = 5$$

If we plot the two points from our example on a coordinate plane and draw a line to connect them, the distance of the line will be 5, and we'll have a triangle!

Slope

If you've gone skiing, you've heard of *slope*. The slope represents the rise of a line (up the y-axis) over its run (across the x-axis). The formula for slope is $\dfrac{(y_2 - y_1)}{(x_2 - x_1)}$, which is the difference of the y variables over the difference of the x variables of two points. The formula $\dfrac{rise}{run}$ is used to plot a line when you have the slope and one of its points.

> *Example:* Find the slope of a line that contains points (1,4) and (3,8).
>
> *Solution:* Plug the two points into the formula: $\dfrac{(8-4)}{(3-1)} = \dfrac{4}{2} = 2$

Not all slopes will equal integers; in fact, most will be fractions. Once you know the slope, you can draw the line to infinity!

> **Just how I was planning on spending my Saturday night—drawing lines to infinity and beyond. How did you guess?**

Midpoint

You can find the *midpoint* of any line segment by adding its endpoints and dividing by 2. The formula for midpoint looks like this: $\left(\dfrac{x_1 + x_2}{2}, \dfrac{y_1 + y_2}{2} \right)$. Again, it looks much nastier than it is. Promise.

Example: Find the midpoint of a line segment with endpoints (–4,1) and (–2,–9).

Solution: Plug in your points and divide each by 2:

$$\left(\frac{-4+(-2)}{2},\frac{1+(-9)}{2}\right)=\left(\frac{-6}{2},\frac{-8}{2}\right)=(-3,-4)$$

A lot of girls at school try to show off their "midpoints" with belly shirts. Personally, I think mystery is much more interesting!

Get Wise!

Try the following coordinate geometry problems.

1. $\overline{AB}$ is the diameter of a circle whose center is O. If the coordinates of A are (2,6) and the coordinates of B are (6,2), find the coordinates of O. (Draw a picture—it's asking for midpoint!)

    (A) (4,4)   (D) (0, 0)

    (B) (4, –4)   (E) (2, 2)

    (C) (2, –2)

2. $\overline{AB}$ is the diameter of a circle whose center is O. If the coordinates of O are (2,1) and the coordinates of B are (4,6), find the coordinates of A.

    (A) $\left(3,3\frac{1}{2}\right)$ (D) $\left(2\frac{1}{2},1\right)$

    (B) $\left(1,2\frac{1}{2}\right)$ (E) $\left(-1,-2\frac{1}{2}\right)$

    (C) (0, –4)

3. The length of the line segment joining the point $A(4,-3)$ to $B(7,-7)$ is

(A) $\sqrt{221}$ (D) $6\frac{1}{2}$

(B) $\sqrt{185}$ (E) 5

(C) 7

4. The vertices of a triangle are $(2,1)$, $(2,5)$, and $(5,1)$. The area of the triangle is
   (A) 12   (D) 6
   (B) 10   (E) 5
   (C) 8

5. The area of a circle whose center is at $(0,0)$ is 16π. The circle passes through each of the following points EXCEPT
   (A) $(4,4)$ (D) $(-4,0)$
   (B) $(0,4)$ (E) $(0,-4)$
   (C) $(4,0)$

How wise? Check your answers on page 232.

VOLUME

Volume is the amount that a three-dimensional object can hold. Say you have a box and want to fill it with sand (or mud, or rose petals, wherever your heart takes you). You need to know the capacity of the box.

I'm always getting yelled at to turn down the volume on the TV or my headphones, but this kind of volume is totally different. And it's easy because it's all just multiplication and there's no yelling involved.

Volume of a Rectangle

The formula for the volume of a rectangle is $V = (l)(w)(h)$.

Example: What is the volume of a rectangular box with length 10, height 5, and width 6?

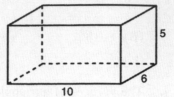

Solution: Draw a box to get a visual:

$$V = (l)(w)(h) = (10)(6)(5) = 300$$

Volume of a Cube

Even easier to find is the volume of a *cube*: All sides are equal, so the length, width, and height are all the same! So, the volume of a cube = s^3.

Example: Find the volume of a cube with side 3.

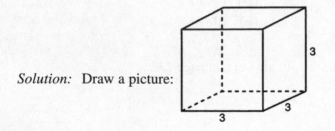

Solution: Draw a picture:

The volume of a cube = s^3 or $(3)^3 = 27$.

Volume of a Cylinder

In a cylinder, you have to take into account that the base is round. So your formula includes some pi and circle stuff mixed in with height:

$$V \text{ of a cylinder} = (\pi)(r^2)(h).$$

Example: Find the volume of a cylinder with radius 4 and height 5.

Solution: Draw a picture:

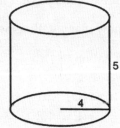

$$V \text{ of a cylinder} = (\pi)(r^2)(h) = (\pi)(16)(5) = 80\pi$$

Three formulas to remember for volume. No problem. Even a goldfish has a memory span of seven minutes.

Get Wise!

Work out each volume problem.

1. The surface area of a cube is 96 square feet (that's the area of ALL six sides). How many cubic feet are there in the volume of the cube? (Volume answers are always in cubic feet!)

   (A) 16   (D) 64

   (B) 4   (E) 32

   (C) 12

2. If the volume of one cube is 8 times as great as another, then the ratio of the area of a face of the larger cube to the area of a face of the smaller cube is

   (A) 2:1   (D) 8:1

   (B) 4:1   (E) $2\sqrt{2}:1$

   (C) $\sqrt{2}:1$

3. A cylindrical pail has a radius of 7 inches and a height of 10 inches. Approximately how many gallons will the pail hold if there are 231 cubic inches to a gallon? $\left(\text{Use } \pi = \dfrac{22}{7}. \right)$

    (A) .9   (D) 5.1
    (B) 4.2   (E) 4.8
    (C) 6.7

4. A rectangular tank 10 inches by 8 inches by 4 inches is filled with water. If the water is to be transferred to smaller tanks in the form of cubes 4 inches on a side, how many of these tanks are needed?

    (A) 4   (D) 7
    (B) 5   (E) 8
    (C) 6

5. The base of a tank is 6 feet by 5 feet and its height is 16 inches. Find the number of cubic feet of water in the tank when it is $\dfrac{5}{8}$ full.

    (A) 25   (D) 768
    (B) 40   (E) 300
    (C) 480

How wise? Check your answers on page 233.

A Word to the Wise

Lines

★ A *line* equals *180 degrees*. Angles next to each other on a line must add up to 180 degrees.

★ *Parallel* lines cut by another line form angles that are related. The big ones are equal and the little ones are equal. *Opposite angles* are always equal.

★ A *bisector* cuts objects into two equal pieces. TIP: Extend the lines to see what angles are equal.

Squares and Rectangles

The Formulas:

★ Perimeter of Rectangle = sum of 4 sides = $l + l + w + w = 2l + 2w$

★ Area of Rectangle = $l \times w$

★ Perimeter of Square = $4s$

★ Area of Square = s^2

★ Squares and rectangles have four 90° angles in each corner. The sum of these four angles is 360°.

Triangles

The Formulas:

★ Perimeter of Triangle = sum of 3 sides

★ Area of Triangle = $\frac{1}{2}bh$

★ *Pythagorean Theorem* for right triangles = $a^2 + b^2 = c^2$, where a and b are sides and c is the hypotenuse.

★ Common *special right triangles* are:

   3–4–5 and doubled 6–8–10

   5–12–13 and doubled 10–24–26

   8–15–17

★ *Equilateral* triangles have three 60-degree angles, and all sides are equal.

   The *altitude* of an equilateral triangle $= \frac{1}{2}$ side $\cdot \sqrt{3}$

30–60–90 Triangles: The Rules

★ The side opposite the 30° angle $= \left(\frac{1}{2}\right) \times$ hypotenuse.

★ The side opposite the 60° angle $= \left(\frac{1}{2}\right)$ (hypotenuse)($\sqrt{3}$).

45–45–90 Triangles: The Rules

★ Each side $= \left(\frac{1}{2}\right)$ (hypotenuse)($\sqrt{2}$)

★ Hypotenuse = (side)($\sqrt{2}$)

★ The *diagonal* of a square forms a 45–45–90 triangle and is therefore equal to a side times $\sqrt{2}$.

★ *Similar* triangles are similar in their proportions.

Circles

The Vocabulary:

- ★ The *radius* is a line from the center to the edge.

- ★ The *diameter* is a line through the center across a circle, which is twice the radius.

The Formulas:

- ★ Diameter = $2r$

- ★ Circumference = πd

- ★ Area = $\pi \cdot r^2$

Coordinate Planes

The Vocabulary:

- ★ Origin is the point (0,0).

- ★ The *x-axis* is a horizontal line. X-coordinates are listed first in the coordinate pair.

- ★ The *y-axis* is a vertical line. Y-coordinates are second in the coordinate pair.

- ★ *Slope* is the value of a line's degree of "steepness."

The Formulas:

- ★ Distance: $\sqrt{(x_2 - x_1)^2 + (y_2 - y_1)^2}$

- ★ Midpoint: $\left(\dfrac{x_1 + x_2}{2}, \dfrac{y_1 + y_2}{2} \right)$

- ★ Slope: $\dfrac{rise}{run}$ or $\dfrac{(y_2 - y_1)}{(x_2 - x_1)}$

Volume

The Formulas:

- ★ *V* of a square = s^3

- ★ *V* of a rectangle = $(l)(w)(h)$

- ★ *V* of a cylinder = $(\pi)(r^2)(h)$

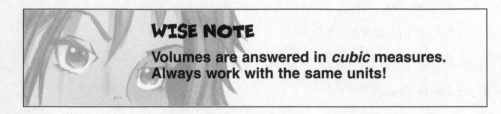

WISE NOTE

**Volumes are answered in *cubic* measures.
Always work with the same units!**

ANSWERS TO CHAPTER 10: PRACTICE EXERCISES

Lines (Page 198)

1. **(A)**

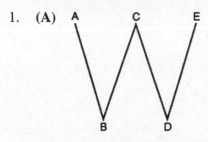

   If angle *B* is 30°, so is angle *D*. Extend the lines in the picture to see what angles are equal.

2. **(D)**

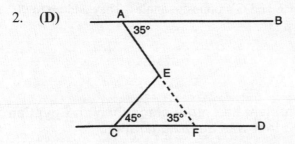

   <u>Extend lines and attack it</u>! Write in all the angle measures you know. The triangle formed has two known angles of 45° and 35°. Since all angles in a triangle add up to 180°, the third angle is 100°. Since the 100-degree angle is next to the only one you want to know, it must equal 80°.

3. **(E)** If angle 1 is 130°, then the angle next to it is 50°. Angle 1 is the "big" one and angle 2 is the "little" one. A line that intersects $\overline{AB}$ will create angles with the same measures because $\overline{AB}$ and $\overline{CD}$ are parallel.

4. **(C)** A bisector must cut the angle in two equal halves. Since the lines are parallel, angles *E* and *G* add up to 180°.

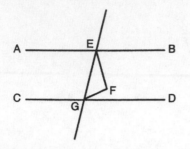

The bisectors both cut *E* and *G*'s opposite angles. Since opposite angles are equal, the sum of *E* and *G*'s opposite angles is also 180. Half of this is 90. Angle *F* is the third angle in a triangle formed by half of each of *E* and *G*'s opposite angles. They add up to 90°, so *F* must also equal 90°.

Geez, this problem had more steps than an Egyptian pyramid! OK, that was an exaggeration.

5. **(C)**

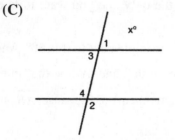

$$\angle 1 = \angle 3$$
$$\angle 2 = \angle 4$$
$$\angle 1 + \angle 2 = \angle 3 + \angle 4$$

It doesn't matter what the value of *x* is; the sum of angles 1 and 2 is 180°.

Squares and Rectangles (Page 201)

1. **(C)** First get the area in square feet. But it wants *yards* so convert it to square yards by dividing by 9. In case you were sleeping, there are 9 square feet in one square yard.

    $(18 \cdot 20) \div 9 = 360 \div 9 = 40$ square yards

2. **(A)** Did you draw it? $A = s^2$

    $$P = 4s$$

    Subtract them!

3. **(D)** The rectangle has an area of 36. If a square has an area of 36, its sides equal 6. *Be careful* now—the problem asks for the perimeter: $6 \times 4 = 24$.

4. **(E)** If you're unsure what the proportions are, don't despair. Just pick 2 dimensions for a rectangle (say, $l = 4$, $w = 3$) and find the area (12). Now double your original proportions ($l = 8$, $w = 6$) and see what you get for a new area (48). How are 12 and 48 related? The new rectangle is four times the original. That's 400%!

Triangles (Page 210)

1. **(D)** If angle $B = x$, then angle A + angle $C = 180 - x$ because all angles must add up to 180°. You also know that $AB = BC$ and you learned if sides are equal, so are their opposite angles. Confused as to which angles these are? No problem—Draw it!

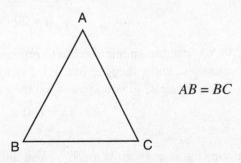

$AB = BC$

2.   **(D)**   Did you notice this was a special right triangle?

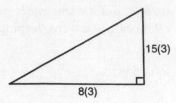

15(3)

8(3)

This is an 8–15–17 triangle with each side multiplied by 3. The missing side is 17(3) = 51.

3.   **(A)**   The diagonal in a square is equal to (side)($\sqrt{2}$). So the side is 6 and the perimeter is 24. Pretty neat how that worked out, eh?

4.   **(C)**   Hopefully, you saw that triangle *ACD* was a special right triangle with dimensions 8, 15, 17. That makes the length of $\overline{CD}$ 8. Now what about the bigger picture? The big triangle *ACB* has sides of 15, 25, and the bottom is unknown. Guess what? The bottom is as easy as a 3–4–5 triangle, because 3, 4, and 5 times 5 is 15, 20, and 25. Remember the long side (hypotenuse) is the side opposite the right angle and the answer in the Pythagoraean Theorem.

But if you didn't see that, you could always use the Pythagorean Theorem to solve for the bottom side, which we'll call *a*:

$$15^2 + a^2 = 25^2$$
$$225 + a^2 = 625$$
$$a^2 = 400$$
$$a = 20$$

5.   **(C)**   You can use simple algebra to represent the lengths of the sides because you know they are in a 1:1:2 ratio. Let them equal *x*, *x*, and 2*x*. It's a triangle, so you know what they add up to:

$$4x = 180$$
$$x = 45$$

So the largest angle is 2*x*, or 90°. (You didn't get tricked and choose (A), did you?)

Circles (Page 215)

1. **(B)** Area of a circle $= \pi r^2$. So the area of a circle with radius x is πx^2. You're told the area is 4.

    $$4 = \pi x^2$$

    You don't need to solve for x, as long as you know that πx^2 is 4.

    Area of a circle with radius $3x$ is $\pi(3x)^2 = 9\pi x^2 = 9 \cdot 4 = 36$.

WISE NOTE

Real numbers are easier to work with than letters (variables). You'll get the same answers; just remember to keep your work organized and write down what numbers you're using for what letters.

2. **(C)** If a side of the square is 6, the diameter is 6 as well! $r = 3$, so $A = \pi \cdot 3^2 = 9\pi$. Shapes in shapes are fun!

3. **(D)** If you don't like algebra mixed in your geometry, use real numbers.

    Say the radius is 5. $C = 10\pi$. Then increase it by 3. $r = 8$, $C = 16\pi$. The circumference increased by 6π. Try it with new numbers if you don't believe us. It works.

4. **(B)** Remember, 30 degrees are between each hour. If the hour hand travels through 4 hours, it has traveled 120 degrees, or one third of the way around. The circle has a radius of 3, so $C = 6\pi$. One third of 6π is 2π.

5. **(E)** One revolution is the circumference $= 36\pi$. Multiply this by 20 $=$ 720π. How many of you were tricked and answered (C)? Your answer here is in inches and the problem asks for *feet*! Divide by 12:

    $$\frac{720}{12} = 60 \text{ feet}$$

Coordinate Planes (Page 218)

1. **(A)** Find the midpoint by averaging the *x*-coordinates and *y*-coordinates:

$$\left(\frac{6+2}{2},\frac{2+6}{2}\right)=(4,4)$$

2. **(C)** Point *O* is the midpoint of segment *AB*. Coordinates of *A* are (*x,y*) below.

    Set up the midpoint formula to equal what you know:

$$\frac{x+4}{2}=2$$
$$x+4=4$$
$$x=0$$

$$\frac{y+6}{2}=1$$
$$y+6=2$$
$$y=-4$$

3. **(E)** Do the distance!

$$d=\sqrt{(7-4)^2+(-7-(-3))^2}$$
$$=\sqrt{(3)^2+(-4)^2}=\sqrt{9+16}$$
$$=\sqrt{25}=5$$

4. **(D)** Plot it! These are only difficult if you don't have straight lines as the sides of the triangle formed. You have straight lines! The altitude is from (2,1) to (2,5) which is up 4 places. The base is from (2,1) over to (5,1), which is 3 places. (Looks like a 3–4–5 triangle . . .) Regardless,

$$A=\frac{1}{2}bh=\frac{1}{2}\cdot 4\cdot 3=6$$

5. **(A)** Draw it if you're unsure! The area is 16π so the radius is 4. The circle is evenly placed 4 points away from the origin (0,0) in all 4

directions. Unless you're an incredibly poor artist, the circle formed would never go through (4,4)!

Volume (Page 221)

1. **(D)** There are 6 equal squares in the surface area of a cube. Each square will have an area of $\dfrac{96}{6}$ or 16. Each edge is 4.

$$V = e^3 = 4^3 = 64$$

2. **(B)** The volume of one cube is 8 times the other. If you dislike algebra, remember you can use your own numbers.

    Volume 1 = 8 (easy one with sides of 2)

    Volume 2 = 64 (easy again, sides are 4)

    So, the ratio of area of big to little is $4 \times 4 : 2 \times 2 = 16 : 4 = 4 : 1$.

    To explain in algebraic terms: The linear ratio is 2:1 so the Area ratio is 4:1.

3. **(C)** $V = \pi r^2 h = \dfrac{22}{7} \cdot 49 \cdot 10 = 1540$ cubic inches

    Divide by 231 to find gallons. Round up to 6.7.

4. **(B)** Find the volume: $10 \times 8 \times 4 = 320$ cubic inches.

    Each cube has a side of 4, so each is 64 cubic inches.

    $\dfrac{320}{64} = 5$ cubes are needed.

5. **(A)** Notice how the height is given in inches and they ask for cubic feet? (If you didn't, then you chose (E), right?) You have to keep units the same!

    16 inches $= 1\dfrac{1}{3} = \dfrac{4}{3}$ feet

Find your volume: $5 \cdot 6 \cdot \dfrac{4}{3} = \dfrac{120}{3} = 40$. But that's when it's *full*. Notice 40 is answer choice (B).

But you need to find $\dfrac{5}{8}$ of the full amount. That requires multiplication (*of* tells us that, remember?):

$$\dfrac{5}{8} \times 40 = 25$$

Congratulations, dear learner, you've reached the end. It's been fun, but seriously, I think you now deserve a break. Before returning to the beginning of the book to ace the problems once again and prove to yourself and your parents that this book was well worth it, go have some ice cream or take a nap. Check you later!